FAMILY BIBLE STORY
# ABRAHAM

Presented to

.........................................................................

by

.........................................................................

on this date

.........................................................................

To order, call

1-800-765-6955.


Visit us at

www.familybiblestory.com

for information on other Review and Herald® products.

# FAMILY BIBLE STORY

# ABRAHAM

*Text by*

## RUTH REDDING BRAND

*Color paintings by* John White

*Pencil Illustrations by* Darrel Tank

REVIEW AND HERALD® PUBLISHING ASSOCIATION
HAGERSTOWN, MD 21740

Pencil Illustrations Copyright © 2004 by Darrel Tank. All Rights Reserved under the Pan-American and International Copyright Conventions.

Bible texts credited to RSV are from the Revised Standard Version of the Bible, copyright © 1946, 1952, 1971, by the Division of Christian Education of the National Council of the Churches of Christ in the U.S.A. Used by permission.

Scriptures credited to ICB are quoted from the *International Children's Bible, New Century Version,* copyright © 1983, 1986, 1988 by Word Publishing, Dallas, Texas 75039. Used by permission.

This book was
Edited by Richard W. Coffen
Copyedited by Jocelyn Fay, Delma Miller, and James Cavil
Designed by Trent Truman
Cover art by John White
Typeset: Galliard 13/22

PRINTED IN U.S.A.

08  07  06  05  04          5  4  3  2  1

**R&H Cataloging Service**
Family Bible Story: Abraham
    V.

    1. Bible Stories.  I. Brand, Ruth Redding

        220.9505

ISBN 0-8280-1856-1 hardcover
ISBN 0-8280-1857-X paperback

# DEDICATED TO

*Gail Hunt—*

artist, designer, musician,
dreamer, genius, and

the inspiration for this book.

# CONTENTS

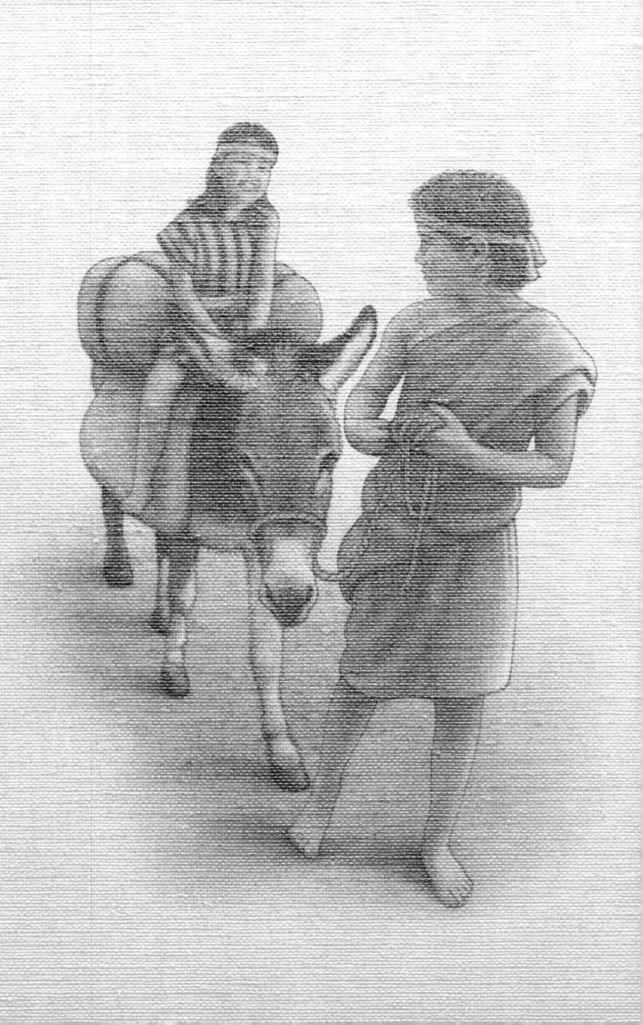

# HOW TO USE THIS BOOK

S it down with this book and a child, and you are creating one of life's rich experiences. Long before children can follow the plot of a story, they can find security in listening to words you share from the pages of a book.

As you begin reading this volume to your children, you are engaging their imagination. The words allow them to create scenes. They are meeting characters they can get to know. They learn more than just the lines they are saying. They learn about what they're thinking and feeling—and they're achieving a vocabulary for expressing thoughts and feelings. They are also learning about families and how they behave.

So you begin a story, and stop at an interesting place. Talk about it—and promise more tomorrow.

Tomorrow, you can let your child tell the story thus far, using the pictures and memory. Offer minimal coaching to the budding storyteller. Then you're ready to continue.

Some stories lend themselves to questions, such as "What would you have done?" Or you might end with a comment, such as "I'd have been scared/excited/uneasy/curious if I'd been there."

Once you have established a Bible story reading ritual, plan to move into a regular family worship and prayertime. Tailor time and topic to the interests and attention span of your child. Begin by reading the story. With preschoolers who are learning language skills, you can talk about the story: What would you do if you had been there? What do you think happened next? What do you suppose _____ expected?

If you would like to start, or resurrect, morning worship for your family, consider one family's formula for success:

**OPENING BLACK & WHITE DRAWING**
Every story will open with a delightful little black-and-white pencil drawing by Darrel Tank.

**THE BIBLE STORIES**
These Bible stories for school-age children were especially written for this new series by Ruth Redding Brand. The stories are all written at a fifth-grade reading level and are designed to be read by children ages 9 through 12.

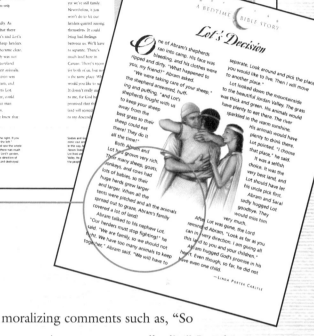

**PHOTOGRAPHS**
These photos of modern sites in Bible lands tie the stories to the same Holy Land that children see on the news each evening.

**THE BIBLE TEXT**
At the bottom of the second spread of each story are the actual Bible verses (from the ICB) on which the story is based. We put them at the bottom of the page because they are the foundation on which the whole series of books is based.

**STORIES FOR PRESCHOOLERS**
These delightful little one-page stories are actually condensed versions of the longer story—written for preschoolers, ages 2-5, and using simple language to retell the same Bible story for little ones.

---

Get up earlier in the morning. This ritual shouldn't replace essentials such as jogging, morning showers, and preparations for school or work. For breakfast, prepare something popular with family members. (In this home, the "specialty" that aroused everyone happily was pumpkin pie.) Awaken family members. Announce time and menu for breakfast (you're a salesperson with a marketable product), and set the stereo on *loud* to fill the house with a lively Mozart or Beethoven symphony. This should arouse slumberers.

Banish all urges to issue instructions, complaints, or naggings at the table. Entertain suggestions for family outings, meals, or hospitality gestures. Breakfast is upbeat. Express thanks for anything you appreciate: promptness, a fragrance worn, or a hair ribbon. The television and radio are off. Engage in significant talk that includes the children. Let them feel their importance to you.

The meal ended, read today's Bible story. Avoid moralizing comments such as, "So you see, it never pays to tell a lie." Let the story carry the power of its thematic development, in the manner of Jesus' stories. On occasions when leisure permits (the school bus is late, you're on vacation, or the weekend has arrived), talk in a nonpatronizing way about what you've read:

Know what I'd have done if I had been there?
Why do you suppose this story is in the Bible?
What kind of friend would _____ be?
What kind of father/mother would _____ be?

When you close worship with prayer, be specific. Pray for family members by name. Prayertime is not the time to preach or instruct—"Help Jody to keep his room neater." It *is* a marvelous time, however, to acknowledge your need for divine power. Can you imagine the impact you're making when your child hears your daily appeal to the Father in heaven for guidance?

On occasions when you are absent for morning or evening worship and family prayers, provide for your children's spiritual nurturing. Get the most out of your babysitting dollars by assigning the sitter to read as you're accustomed to do when you put the children to bed. (An ingenious parent doesn't countenance unsupervised television viewing by children. If ever they need your guidance and feedback, it's when they are watching commercial television. Sit through it with them; don't allow someone whose values you don't admire to program your child's visual menu. Your feedback after a program is crucial.)

If you're planning an extended trip, tape-record stories in sequence from this book, an excellent way to let the children hear your voice each day and to let them know you remember them. They can follow along "reading" the pictures while your familiar voice provides the narrative.

If television is competing for book time in your family (do you really want your children to spend more time in front of the tube than they spend in learning and physical activities?), move in to take charge. Jim Trelease tells about announcing to his family that the TV would be quiet on all school nights—forever. The protest and complaints that ensued lasted three months, he admits. But his strong conviction that television was robbing his children of important experiences caused him to remain adamant. He says that the children now may choose one special program during the week to watch. This process makes them much more discriminating about quality programs. And they have both time and appetite for formerly neglected activities. (See Jim Trelease, *The Read-Aloud Handbook* [Penguin, 1982], pp. 98, 99.)

John Adams, writing in 1765, noted that "a native American who cannot read . . . is as rare an appearance . . . as a comet or an earthquake." Anthony Brandt attributes this verbal competence to the fact that the colonial child was exposed from infancy to the family's daily oral Bible reading. (See Anthony Brandt, "Literacy in America," New York *Times,* Aug. 25, 1980, p. 25.)

On the average, today's youth are not so literate as their forefathers. The current decline in achievement among school children noted in the United States parallels the rise in television viewing, which seems to dim the inclination to read. A half million students in grades 6 to 12 taking achievement tests in 1980 answered a question in the heart of the test: How many hours do you spend watching television? The results showed that the more students watched television, the lower their achievement scores tended to be, even when their scores were corrected for IQ, study habits, and socioeconomic background. (See Trelease, p. 93.)

Children whose parents model reading and who read to them today are blessed. These children get the idea that books are part of life and are to be pursued.

Parents who plan a library for their children usually include some inexpensive, indestructible books that remain within the child's reach. They also provide an out-of-reach shelf—it could be high on the wall in the child's room—where the read-aloud books appear. These books provide a goal for small children. They get to look at them with Mom and Dad. These special books enhance waking up and going to sleep times. That special shelf for special books is the place for this volume and its companions while your children wait to achieve the skills to read for themselves.

The age-old appeal of stories inside this book's cover beckons. Sit down with the children for whom you selected this book. Add dimensions to their world by choosing a compelling story that builds confidence in a Supreme Being. Look for that theme in every story from the Book of books.

—EDNA MAYE LOVELESS

## Timeline (above)

- Abram born (2166 B.C.)
- Sarah born (2155 B.C.)

- Peleg dies (2117 B.C.?)
- Nahor dies (2116 B.C.)
- Noah dies (2107 B.C.?)
- Abram leaves Haran (2091 B.C.)

- Abram enters Canaan (2091 B.C.)
- Lot captured (2086 B.C.)
- Abram marries Hagar (2080 B.C.)
- Ishmael born (2079 B.C.?)
- Isaac born; Abraham 100 years old (2066 B.C.)

- Isaac offered at Mount Moriah (2045 B.C.)
- Sarah dies (2028 B.C.)
- Isaac marries Rebekah (2026 B.C.)
- Jacob & Esau born (2006 B.C.)
- Abraham dies (1991 B.C.) at 175 years of age

**B.C.    2200    /  /  /    2150    /  /  /    2100    /  /  /    2050    /  /  /    2000**

- Nannepadda, high priestess of Sin (moon god) at Ur (2163 B.C.)
- Ur-Baba, king of Lagash (2155 B.C.)
- Drought collapses Egyptian Old Kingdom

- Gudea is king of Lagash (2141)
- Yu the Great, legendary founder of China's Xia Dynasty (2120)
- Ziggurat at Ur built
- Pottery from Parita Bay area of Panama
- Ur-Nammu becomes king of Ur (2112 B.C.)
- Invention of 360° circle

- Ur-Nammu dies (2095)
- Ur no longer capital city of Neo-Sumerian Empire
- Princess Imertnebes of Thebes, Egypt, called "God's Wife of Amon"

- Third dynasty of Assyria flourishes (2030 B.C.)
- First zoo—in China (c. 2000 B.C.)
- First sails used—by Phoenicians (c. 2000 B.C.)
- Chess invented in Persia (c. 2000 B.C.)

## ABRAHAM

Born in the city of Ur, Abram later moved to Haran. When he was 75 years old, God told Abram to leave for an unknown land—the "promised land." When he was 100 years old, his son Isaac was born. Abraham died at 175 years of age. Scripture refers to him as God's friend (2 Chronicles 20:7; compare Isaiah 41:8).

## SARAI/SARAH

Sarah, the half sister and wife of Abraham, was 10 years younger than he. She was legendary for her beauty. Sarah was 90 when she gave birth to Isaac. She died when she was 127 years old. Abraham buried her in the Cave of Machpelah. The names Sarai and Sarah are closely related to each other, and both mean "princess."

## LOT

Lot was the son of Abram's brother Haran. Lot accompanied Abram on the trip to Canaan. Lot came to own large flocks and had many servants. When God decided to destroy the city of Sodom, Lot, his wife, and two unmarried daughters fled Sodom, but his wife turned around to look at the city and turned into a "pillar of salt."

## HAGAR

Hagar, Sarah's Egyptian maidservant, was probably just a young girl when Sarah acquired her. When aged Sarah had not given birth to the promised son, she told 85-year-old Abraham to take Hagar as a concubine so that a son could be born to Abraham, if not to both Abraham and Sarah. Hagar gave birth to Ishmael.

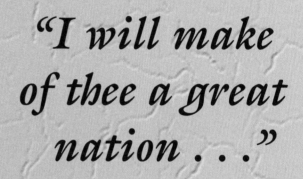

# "I will make of thee a great nation . . ."

*Genesis 12:2*

# GOING TO THE PROMISED LAND

Life in Haran was good to Abram and all his family. Their flocks and herds grew fat and healthy. People were friendly to Abram and his nephew Lot. Haran wasn't exactly like Ur, the city they had left years earlier, but it was a pleasant place. There was one big difference. Abram had now many animals, so they lived outside the city—in tents, mind you! Sarai surprised herself by beginning to enjoy life in a tent, for it was easy to care for and could be opened to the air or closed for privacy.

One day, with his family around him, father Terah died. Abram felt sad. He knew he would miss Terah, but something else made him happy. He would be able to move on to Canaan, as God had told him to do when they had lived in Ur.

Abram had never forgotten the reason he had left Ur. He told all his new friends about the God who talked to him. Some of them began to worship the Creator-God along with their other gods. They didn't realize that He is the only God.

It had been a long time since God had first talked to Abram. Sometimes Abram would wonder, just a bit, if God still wanted him to move on. Then one starry night Abram walked outside alone, listening to the noises of the night. He heard the gentle sounds of his flocks and herds. There were soft thuds as bodies shifted position;

munching sounds as animals chewed their cuds; low moos as cows called to their calves. In the distance the howl of a wolf and the cry of an eagle owl pierced the still night air.

Then out of the stillness came a voice, a voice that he had been listening for. "Leave your country, your relatives and your father's family," God told him. "Go to the land I will show you. I will make you a great nation, and I will bless you. I will make you famous. And you will be a blessing to others."[1]

Abram sang as he ran all the way back to Sarai's tent. "Sarai! Sarai!" he called.

Sarai whirled round and stared at Abram. "What? What is it?" she gasped.

"He talked to me again! He talked to me again! The God who told us to leave Ur and go to Canaan! Oh, Sarai, we must get

This ostrich-egg jar was uncovered in a royal tomb at Ur by archaeologist Sir Charles Leonard Woolley. It probably dates from the time of Abram's grandfather.

ready! He said we must leave Haran."

Sarai looked at Abram. She had nearly forgotten that they had stopped in Haran only because Terah could not travel farther. Even though they were renting land and living in a tent here, Haran now felt very much like home.

"Just what did God say to you?" she asked quietly.

Breathlessly, Abram told her. Sarai turned the words over in her mind: *Go to the land I will show you. I will make you a great nation. . . . I will make you famous.*

What would this land look like? Would it truly be theirs? And how would Abram become a great nation? He would have to have children, and . . . Sarai again looked at Abram's shining face. This God who spoke to him seemed to know all about them and care about them. They would go to Canaan!

## MOVING DAY

Abram planned the trip so that they would leave in the spring, heading for the high pastures, still green from the winter rains. Once more donkeys were loaded with blankets and tents and cooking pots and bundles of barley and wheat. Once more all the animals were rounded up and all the people gathered together. But this time Terah was not there. Abram stood in his place.

Abram looked around him. Hundreds of people would be going with him. And although God had told Abram to leave his relatives behind, his nephew Lot, now all grown up, would also go with them. Again Abram glanced at Sarai, grown even more beautiful with the passing of time.

With a glad cry Abram gave the command to move, and the great line of people and animals surged forward. Abram had carefully chosen the route they would take. This time they would not be traveling through a river valley, even though water—water for thirsty animals—was even more important than food

**GENESIS 12:1-9**

Then the Lord said to Abram, "Leave your country, your relatives and your father's family. Go to the land I will show you.

"I will make you a great nation, and I will bless you. I will make you famous. And you will be a blessing to others. I will bless those who bless you. I will place a curse on those who harm you. And all the people on earth will be blessed through you."

So Abram left Haran as the Lord had told him. And Lot went with him. At this time Abram was 75 years old. Abram took his wife Sarai, his nephew Lot and everything they owned. They took all the servants they had gotten in Haran. They set out from Haran, planning to go to the land of Canaan. In time they arrived there.

or shelter. Instead he picked a route that brought them to the few wells and springs scattered along the way. These sources of fresh water were carefully guarded. And Sarai smiled with pride as she saw how polite and skillful Abram was as he bargained with those who claimed the water wells as theirs. He would bend low and greet them, inquire of their health, offer them presents. Then permission would be given to use the well, and the women would let down the leather buckets, bringing them up spilling and sloshing with the sparkling water. As they poured it into troughs, the animals would break into a run, jostling each other to be first to drink. Women passed around goatskin bags with cool, wet water.

Day after day the caravan journeyed on. Donkeys, goats, sheep, cows, and people plodded on, traveling from five to seven miles each day. Then one day green fields

Water was not always easily found in Caanan. Towns were built up around natural springs. Otherwise, people dug wells and cisterns.

appeared. A river and groves of trees offered relief to the sun-seared eyes of the travelers. Then the walls of a city loomed before them, and Abram's family entered the exciting city of Damascus.

But Damascus was not their destination. Once

more they journeyed, traveling south. Green fields behind them, they trudged across empty, lifeless plains dotted with dry grass.

Now the country was becoming less flat. Wadis (dry riverbeds) ran toward the Jordan River.

Abram traveled through that land. He went as far as the great tree of Moreh at Shechem. The Canaanites were living in the land at that time. The Lord appeared to Abram. The Lord said, "I will give this land to your descendants." So Abram built an altar there to the Lord, who had appeared to him. Then Abram traveled from Shechem to the mountain east of Bethel. And he set up his tent there. Bethel was to the west, and Ai was to the east. There Abram built another altar to the Lord and worshiped him. After this, he traveled on toward southern Canaan.

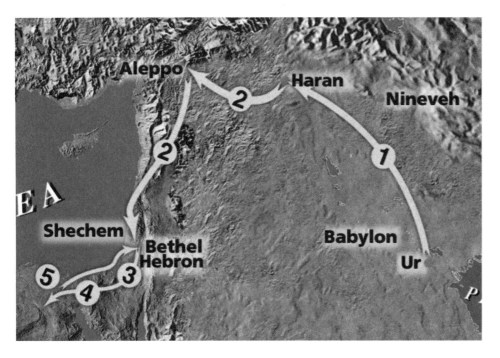

**ABRAM'S JOURNEYS**
(1) Abram moved from Ur to Haran; (2) from Haran Abram moved to Canaan; (3) he stopped at Shechem, Bethel, and the Negeb; (4) when famine hit, he moved to Egypt; and (5) at the end of the famine Abram moved back to Canaan.

and deep wadis cutting their way to the sea. Was this the land God had promised him?

Wisely staying in the highlands, Abram took his clan into a valley between Mount Ebal and Mount Gerazim, to a place called Shechem.

There, once more, God spoke to Abram. "I will give this land to your descendants."[2] What a wonderful time for God to speak again to Abram! What a wonderful promise! Land, this land, promised to a stranger who had no home. And "descendants," children and grandchildren! God promised children to this 75-year-old man who had none!

In joy and thankfulness Abram built an altar to the Lord. Calling his family together, he offered a sacrifice to show God that he trusted Him and would continue to do whatever He asked.

For a while Abram and his family stayed in Shechem, then, needing to find more grazing land, they again headed south. At a place called Bethel they pitched their tents and grazed their flocks. Once again Abram built an altar to the Lord.

People watched as Abram built his altars and offered sacrifices to the God in heaven. They saw something they had never seen before, a man forming a friendship with a God.

Forested hills loomed in the west. With his mind on God, Abram directed his caravan into one of the wadis. Straight toward the Jordan they walked. Then straight into the Jordan River they waded, and when they reached the other side they were in Canaan.

Bushes and trees covered the hills around them. Valleys stretched below them, still blooming with springtime green.

Abram and his company gazed upward at the dry hills crowned with scraggly trees. Other travelers had told them that the other side of these hills was thickly forested. God had given them a land with lots of room in which they could grow.

But Abram and his family were not the only people in this new land. Abram saw a number of walled cities. He saw tribes with weapons for making war. He saw broken-down walls where some tribes had been fighting with others over land and power. He saw hills overrun with thorny plants, valleys filled with stony ground,

---

[1]Genesis 12:1, 2, ICB.
[2]Verse 7, ICB.

# Going to the Promised Land

"Sarai!" Abram exclaimed. "God spoke to me!"

Sarai looked up with wide eyes. "What did He say?" she whispered.

"God told me to leave this country," Abram answered. "God said to go to another land that He will show me. God said He will make me the father of a great nation, and that He will bless me and make me a blessing to others."

Abram sat down to think about all the big things God had said.

Sarai looked around at her pretty tent home, and a tear slipped down her cheek. It would be so hard to leave her home! It would be so hard to leave her friends and her relatives. But of course Abram would do what God had commanded. And of course she would go with him.

So Sarai packed, and Abram planned. It took a long time to get ready to go. Sarai bought more tents for the trip, and Abram bought sacks and sacks of grain to make into bread along the way. Sarai tried to decide which of her favorite things she would take with her, and Abram organized all the servants who would help care for his herds of sheep and goats and cows and donkeys on the trip. Abram's nephew, Lot, decided to go with Uncle Abram too.

It was a long, long trip to the Promised Land. Abram's family traveled hundreds of miles. It was a slow trip. The animals had to graze and rest.

Finally Abram reached his new home-land, Canaan. And the Lord appeared to him there. "I am going to give this land to your children and your children's children!" He said to Abram.

Abram joyfully built an altar and thanked and worshipped the Lord. And He hugged God's promise in his heart, even though, so far, he did not have a child.

—Linda Porter Carlyle

# LOT'S DECISION

Abram thought a lot about the God of heaven. More and more he realized that the God of Noah and Enoch was not just another God. He was *the* God. The *only* God. He was a God one could turn to in Ur, or Haran, or Canaan, or Egypt. The Creator-God was everywhere. And He was more powerful than a king, more loving than a family, more wise than any person.

Now it seemed that all was well. Abram was at peace with God. The animals had plenty to eat and drink. Sarai sang softly as she worked a stone mill round and round, grinding barley into flour. Abram had pitched camp in the Promised Land.

As he stood outside his goat-hair tent, he looked at one of the strangest gifts he had ever received. The Egyptian pharaoh had given it to him. This "gift" stood on four knobby-kneed legs. Its body was humped up in a strange way on its back. Its long neck supported a head that looked something like a goat's, something like a donkey's, and something like that of a stuck-up woman.

It peered down at Abram from under its heavy eyelids, and it had pulled back its lips in what looked like a scornful smile. Pharaoh had given Abram a camel, actually several camels, which people were just beginning to use for carrying packs. Abram had been amazed on the journey out of Egypt at how little water the camels needed to drink.

Abram smiled up at the camel. "You sure are the strangest-looking thing!" he murmured. Suddenly one of his best herdsmen stood before him. It was odd that he would appear now. He should have been in the fields with the cattle.

"What's wrong?" asked Abram.

"Sir, everything is wrong!" the herdsman cried. "I was grazing my herds peacefully when all of a sudden one of Lot's herdsmen appeared with his cattle, and they started grazing on the same pasture-land. Soon all the grass was gone. I took my herds to another area where we have grazed before, but some of Lot's shepherds moved there with their flocks. I can't go down into the valleys any farther than I have, because of the Canaanites and the Perizzites with their flocks. If something isn't done . . ."

While the faithful herder was still speaking, Lot appeared. He looked upset. "Uncle Abram," he said, "we need to talk."

The herdsman politely left Abram so that uncle and nephew might talk privately. The two men looked at each other. Abram spoke first. "I understand that we have some trouble."

Although God promised to give Abram the whole land of Canaan, the only real estate he ever owned was the Cave of Machpelah, a tomb, which is located inside this building.

## "THERE'S ROOM FOR BOTH OF US, BUT NOT IN THE SAME PLACE. WHERE WOULD YOU LIKE TO SETTLE?"

"Yes, Uncle," Lot answered respectfully. As they talked, they both began to realize that there had been many squabbles among Abram's and Lot's cattle and sheep herders. One thing became clear. There simply was not enough pastureland for all of their animals.

The solution was plain to Abram, and it was plain to Lot. Lot, however, could not suggest that they part ways. The older man must suggest the answer to their problem.

Abram smiled sadly at his nephew. He knew that

**GENESIS 13:5-18**

During this time Lot was traveling with Abram. Lot also had many sheep, cattle and tents. Abram and Lot had so many animals that the land could not support both of them together. Abram's herders and Lot's herders began to argue. The Canaanites and the Perizzites were living in the land at this time.

So Abram said to Lot, "There should be no arguing between you and me. Your herders and mine should not argue either. We are brothers. We should separate. The whole land is there in front of you. If you go to the left, I will go to the right. If you go to the right, I will go to the left."

Lot looked all around and saw the whole Jordan Valley. He saw that there was much water there. It was like the Lord's garden, like the land of Egypt in the direction of Zoar. (This was before the Lord destroyed they must part. Lot had his own family now. He had his flocks and herds, but not enough land on which to feed them. It was time to say goodbye, but, oh, it was so hard. Abram had loved Lot like a son ever since Lot had been a little boy.

"Lot," he spoke gently, "you're no longer a child. You are not dependent on me, yet we're still family. Nevertheless, it just won't do to let our herders quarrel among themselves. It could bring bad feelings between us. We'll have to separate. There's much land here in Canaan. There's room for both of us, but not in the same place. Where would you like to settle? It doesn't really matter to me, for God has promised that this whole land will someday belong to my descendants."

# CAMELS

Did you know that there are two kinds of camels? The Bactrian camel has two humps and lives where winters are cold, as in Mesopotamia and central Asia—the land Abram/Abraham left behind. The bigger dromedary, or Arabian camel, has one hump and thrives in warm climates such as Arabia, Egypt, and Palestine. Dromedaries have a range of colors that go from white to nearly black.

Camels have two toes, slits for nostrils (which they can close during a sandstorm), and double rows of eyelashes to keep sand from hurting their eyes. Camels store fat—not water—in the hump, which can hold as much as 80 pounds of fat. Camels use water efficiently and in cool weather can go as long as 25 days before drinking. When thirsty, camels can drink 100 quarts of water in just 10 minutes!

Despite being shorter and stockier than the dromedary, a Bactrian camel can carry heavier loads. Although a camel can carry up to 600 pounds for short distances, it does better carrying about 300 pounds.

Bactrian camels can walk nearly three miles an hour. Dromedaries can walk seven to eight miles per hour for 18-hour stretches. Some dromedary camels are bred for speed and can sprint at 10 miles an hour. An able camel rider can travel 60 to 75 miles in a day. Aside from biblical stories that mention someone riding a camel, the clearest and earliest evidence of camel riding comes from *Tell el-Halaf* in Mesopotamia around the tenth century B.C.

The earliest mention of camels in written records comes from an inscription of Assur-bal-Kala (1074 to 1057 B.C.) in Assyria. Authorities differ on when the camel was first tamed and used as a pack animal. There seems to be some evidence that during the first dynasty of Egypt, during the fourth millennium, camels were used. According to Genesis 12 a pharaoh gave some camels to Abram sometime during the late twenty-first century B.C.

The English word "camel" comes from the Greek and Latin word *kamēlos*, which comes from the Hebrew word *gamal*.

© PHOTODISC

Sodom and Gomorrah.) So Lot chose to move east and live in the Jordan Valley. In this way Abram and Lot separated. Abram lived in the land of Canaan. But Lot lived among the cities in the Jordan Valley. He moved very near to Sodom. Now the people of Sodom were very evil. They were always sinning against the Lord.

After Lot left, the Lord said to Abram, "Look all around you. Look north and south and east and west. All this land that you see I will give to you and your descendants forever. I will make your descendants as many as the dust of the earth. If anyone could count the dust on the earth, he could count your people. Get up! Walk through all this land. I am now giving it to you."

So Abram moved his tents. He went to live near the great trees of Mamre. This was at the city of Hebron. There he built an altar to the Lord.

The word *Jordan* means "descender," a good description of this river that begins in the mountains and ends in the Dead Sea. The river

It took a lot of faith for Abram to think that way, for he was no longer young, and he had no descendants at all. Lot knew about the promise to Abram, and he believed it also.

Where Abram and Lot stood, they had a good view of the valley that stretched out below them to the horizon. Lot gazed at the Jordan River valley, deciding that it was a good place to get rich. The Bible tells us that the land had plenty of water, and water meant wealth. Compared to the rocky hills and desert land around it, the Jordan River valley looked like the Garden of Eden! Then, too, it reminded Lot of the land he had left as a child, the fertile plains

and marshes of southern Mesopotamia.

Lot should have said, "Uncle Abram, you choose first." That was the polite thing to do.

And Uncle Abram would have replied, "No. You choose first."

Lot would have answered, "Far be it from *me* to make the first choice. *You* must do it, Uncle Abram." The two men would continue negotiating back and forth before Abram would have made the decision.

But that's not what happened. Lot selfishly chose for himself the land that looked best, the land that had the river, the land green with shrubs and reeds and trees. After having made his decision, Lot moved

flows through part of the Great Rift Valley of Africa, which extends some 4,000 miles. The winding river itself flows for about 200 miles.

east so that he could live nearby the green strip of vegetation growing along the banks of the Jordan River. And Abram went the other direction.

There was one big problem, though. Located in this same area that Lot had chosen were the cities of Sodom and Gomorrah. These cities had a bad reputation. The Bible says that the people who lived there "were very evil. They were always sinning against the Lord."[1] Despite their wickedness, Lot moved into this area—"very near to Sodom."[2] (He later moved into the city of Sodom.)

Lot probably didn't realize what an important decision he was making when he chose the place where he would establish his family. He certainly could not look ahead and see what troubles would come to him after he left Abram.

But there were some things that Lot could have thought about. He could have thought about how God had blessed Abram, making him a rich man. Yet it had never been Abram's purpose to get rich. Abram's purpose in life was to serve God. Lot could have thought about the good influence Abram had been on him while he was growing up. What kind of influence would the wicked people of Sodom have on him and his family? He could have thought of how unselfish Abram had always been and how unselfish he was even now. He might even have thought about giving Abram the first choice of a place to live, even though God had promised it all to Abram anyway.

Lot would have reasons to think about those things in the days to come, but as he hugged Abram and Sarai and told them goodbye, he felt excited. He would be on his own. Already rich, thanks to the kindness of Abram, he dreamed of becoming even richer. Someday he would be a great and mighty chieftain!

Sadly Abram and Sarai watched Lot and all his family and servants and goats and sheep and cattle and donkeys move away. They knew they would see him again, because the Jordan Valley was not that far distant, but never again would Lot be part of their family in quite the same way that he had been.

Then God spoke again to Abram. "Abram," He said, "look all around you. Look north and south and east and west. All this land that you see I will give to you and your descendants forever."[3]

Once again the promise had been given! Land . . . children. Although Abram pitched his tents and grazed his flocks and herds in the land of Canaan, he still owned not one speck of land. And he still had no children. But God had promised! And Abram believed.

He moved his tents south to a place called Hebron. There, on the oak-covered hillsides, Abram felt at home. Once more his flocks and herds grazed peacefully. Gone was the strife between his herders and Lot's. Gone, too, was Lot. Abram missed him, but he knew that God would watch over Lot just as He had watched over him and Sarai for so many years.

Abram built an altar to the Lord. Calling his large household around, Abram once more worshipped the God of heaven.

---

[1]Genesis 13:13, ICB.
[2]Verse 12, ICB.
[3]Verses 14, 15, ICB.

The Jordan River valley itself is about 70 miles long. The deltas, formed where the tributaries flow into the Jordan, are especially fertile.

# Lot's Decision

One of Abram's shepherds ran into camp. His face was bleeding, and his clothes were ripped and dirty. "What happened to you, my friend?" Abram asked.

"We were taking care of your sheep," the shepherd answered, huffing and puffing, "and Lot's shepherds fought with us to keep your sheep away from the best grass so their sheep could eat there! They do it all the time!"

Both Abram and Lot had grown very rich. Their many sheep, goats, donkeys, and cows had lots of babies, so their huge herds grew larger and larger. When all the tents were pitched and all the animals spread out to graze, Abram's family covered a lot of land!

Abram talked to his nephew Lot. "Our herders must stop fighting!" he said. "We are family, so we should not fight. We have too many animals to keep together," Abram said. "We will have to separate. Look around and pick the place you would like to live. Then I will move to another place."

Lot looked down the mountainside to the beautiful Jordan Valley. The grass was thick and green. His animals would have plenty to eat there. The river sparkled in the warm sunshine. His animals would have plenty to drink there. Lot pointed. "I choose that place," he said.

It was a selfish choice. It was the very best land, and Lot should have let his uncle pick first.

Sadly Abram and Sarai hugged Lot goodbye. They would miss him very much.

After Lot was gone, the Lord reminded Abram, "Look as far as you can in every direction. I am giving all this land to you and your children."

Abram hugged God's promise in his heart, even though, so far, he did not have even one child.

—LINDA PORTER CARLYLE

# STARS AND BIRDS AND FIREPOTS

Do you remember the last dream you had? Was it silly? Was it scary? Did something nice happen in your dream?

Perhaps you don't remember dreaming at all. People often forget their dreams, but everyone dreams, every night. Usually dreams are not very important, but once in a while they are.

God sometimes gives a very special kind of dream to some people. A person doesn't even have to be sleeping to have this unusual kind of dream. The dream that God gives to people is called a vision. And when God gives a vision to someone, it is important.

Sarai noticed that Abram grew more and more quiet with each day that passed. But now something was on his mind. "Abram!" she called softly one day. But Abram just stared straight ahead, as if he hadn't even heard her. "Abram!" Sarai called again, louder this time.

With a start Abram turned to her. "Yes, sorry, what is it?"

"Abram, where were you? What do you think about when you grow so quiet and look off into space? Is something troubling you?"

Abram cleared his throat and shrugged his shoulders. He didn't know what to say. How could he tell Sarai that with each passing day, month, and year he saw God's promise of

children growing fainter and fainter? He knew how Sarai had suffered all these years because she had no children. Other women laughed at her and said she was no good because she hadn't given her husband even one son. Not having any children, especially not having a son, was often seen as a curse, but God had promised to bless Abram. Abram refused to add his worries to Sarai's grief.

Besides, having a son meant keeping one's name "alive." A son would bring honor to his father and mother while the parents were alive. And after his parents' death he would give a kind of "immortality" to the father by perpetuating the father's honor and name.

But something else bothered Abram. Even if God's promise of children did come true, what did he have for his son to inherit? Yes, he owned many flocks and herds and had much silver and gold, but he still owned not a patch of land in all of Canaan. And land was important to people living in the ancient Near East. It endured. Animals died. Gold and silver could be lost or traded. But land—land was permanent. Land brought security.

How could God's promises come true when Abram had no children and did not own an acre of land? Abram desperately wanted to believe God's promises. In fact, he did believe God's promises, but questions kept repeating in his mind: *When? How?*

But Abram didn't want to bother his wife with these questions, so he gave her an absentminded hug, then left her tent, seeking his own. He needed to be alone with God.

God understood Abram's thoughts and chose this moment, when Abram most needed encouragement, to reassure him. Suddenly Abram heard God's voice in a vision. That voice, loud as thunder but sweet as music, was one that Abram knew right away, even though he had not heard it for many years. "Abram," said God, "don't be afraid. I will defend you. And I will give you a great reward."

"Lord God," Abram complained, "what can you give me? I have no son."

But Abram had made plans—perhaps to help God out, to help God keep His promise. So he continued, "My slave Eliezer from Damascus will get everything I own after I die."

Abram, in his vision, paused. But God made no answer. He knew Abram wanted to say more. So Abram plunged ahead. "Look, you have given me no son. So a slave born in my house will inherit everything I have."[1] Eliezer, Abram's servant, would become Abram's legal heir. That's the way it was done at that time when someone did not have a flesh-and-blood son.

Then God spoke, His words solemn and sure.

> "THERE ARE SO MANY STARS YOU CANNOT COUNT THEM. YOUR DESCENDANTS WILL BE TOO MANY TO COUNT."

---

**GENESIS 15:1-18**

The Lord spoke . . . to Abram. . . . "Abram, don't be afraid. I will defend you. And I will give you a great reward." But Abram said, "Lord God, what can you give me? I have no son. So my slave Eliezer from Damascus will get everything I own after I die." . . .

Then the Lord spoke . . . to Abram. . . . "That slave will not be the one to inherit what you have. You will have a son of your own. And your son will inherit what you have." Then God led Abram outside. God said, "Look at the sky. There are so many stars you cannot count them. And your descendants will be too many to count." . . .

But Abram said, "Lord God, how can I be sure that I will own this land?" The Lord said to Abram, "Bring me a three-year-old cow, a three-year-old goat

God told Abram that his descendants would be like the stars—too many to count. A few thousand stars are visible at night, and there are 100 to 300 billion stars in our Milky Way Galaxy.

"Eliezer will not be the one to inherit what you have."

God took Abram by the hand and led him out under the night sky. Have you ever been out in the country and looked at the sky on a clear night? If you have, you know how brightly the stars can shine when the air is clean. In Canaan, thousands of years

and a three-year-old male sheep. Also bring me a dove and a young pigeon."

Abram brought them all to God. Then Abram killed the animals and cut each of them into two pieces. He laid each half opposite the other half. But he did not cut the birds in half. Later, large birds flew down to eat the ani-

mals. But Abram chased them away.

As the sun was going down, Abram fell into a deep sleep. While he was asleep, a very terrible darkness came. Then the Lord said to Abram, "You can be sure that your descendants will be strangers and travel in a land they don't own. . . . Abram, you

will live to be very old. . . ."

The sun went down, and it was very dark. Suddenly a smoking firepot and a blazing torch passed between the halves of the dead animals. So on that day the Lord made an agreement with Abram. The Lord said, "I will give this land to your descendants."

# ANCIENT NEAR EASTERN COVENANTS

In a covenant two parties made mutual promises that governed how they would relate to each other.

A typical covenant during the fourteenth and thirteenth centuries B.C. more or less utilized the following pattern.

**1. Identification of the Covenant Maker**—"These are the words of the Sun Mursilis, . . . the king of the Hatti land, the valiant" (*Ancient Near Eastern Texts*, p. 203).

**2. Historical Prologue**—The covenant maker reviews their history with the vassal, emphasizing cordial past relationships. "Aziras was the grandfather of you, Duppi-Tessub. . . . [He] remained loyal toward my father. . . . When your father died, . . . I did not drop you. . . . You were sick and ailing, but . . . I . . . put you in the place of your father" (*ibid.*, pp. 203, 204).

**3. Stipulations**—The covenant maker issues "laws" that protect his interests—often in an "if . . . then . . ." format. "If anyone utters words unfriendly toward the king of the Hatti land before you, Duppi-Tessub, you shall not withhold his name from the king" (*ibid.*, p. 204).

**4. Provision for Deposit**—Copies of the covenant were stored in special locations and periodically

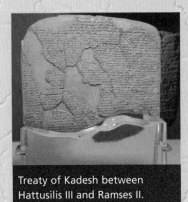

Treaty of Kadesh between Hattusilis III and Ramses II.

taken out for public reading. "A duplicate of this tablet has been deposited before the Sun-goddess of Arinna" (*ibid.*, p. 205).

**5. List of Witnesses**—Honorable witnesses testified to the enactment. "The Sun-god of Heaven, the Sun-goddess of Arinna, . . . the Storm-god of Nuhassi; . . . Sin, lord of the oath, . . . Ishtar of Nineveh, . . . the mountains, the rivers, the springs, the great Sea, heaven and earth, the winds (and) the clouds—let these be witnesses" (*ibid.*).

**6. Enumeration of Blessings and Cursings**—We might call these the "teeth" of the treaty, which gave it staying power. "Should Duppi-Tessub not honor these words . . . , may these gods of the oath destroy Duppi-Tessub. . . . But if Duppi-Tessub honors these words, . . . may these gods . . . protect him together with his person, his wife, his son, his grandson, his house (and) his country" (*ibid.*).

**7. Ratification of the Covenant**—Often an animal was cut into pieces. This sacrifice served as a nonverbal oath that indicated "May what has happened to this animal happen to me if I break covenant." Often a meal followed, with the covenant parties dining on the slaughtered animal.

ago, no cars or buses or factories or burning rubbish heaps polluted the air. No brightly lit cities faded the black velvet skies when Abram walked beneath them long ago.

And now God told Abram to look up at that starry sky. Countless stars blazed in the heavens, and they seemed close enough to touch. "Look at the sky," God told Abram. "There are so many stars you cannot count them."

Abram gazed up at the star-spangled sky. Stars, big as torches, surrounded themselves with hundreds and even thousands of smaller stars. The longer Abram looked, the more stars he saw.

Then God promised, "Your descendants will be too many to count."

A great calm, a deep happiness, welled up in Abram like a spring that never runs dry. He believed God's words and trusted Him.

God continued, "I am the Lord who led you out of Ur of Babylonia. I did that so I could give you this land to own."

Eagerly Abram asked, "How can I be sure that I will own this land?"

God quickly replied, "Bring me a three-year-old cow, a three-year-old goat and a three-year-old male sheep. Also bring one dove and a young pigeon."[2]

Abram's vision ended, but he knew exactly what God had in mind. God planned to make him an unchangeable promise, just as lawyers write legal contracts for people today. Many times Abram had seen animals killed to seal a contract, an agreement between people. No laws enforced by police officers made people keep their word to each other in those days, but people had their own way of making sure a contract was not broken. In this instance God asked Abram to kill some animals and slice them in two lengthwise. God would later do something surprising with these sacrifices.

## FIRE AND SMOKE

Abram obeyed immediately. He killed the animals and cut all the large ones in half. Suddenly from out of the still air came a great flapping of wings and the hoarse screeching of vultures. Swooping toward the butchered animals, wings spread wide and naked heads thrust forward, they grabbed at the meat with their powerful beaks. Desperately Abram picked up stones, a branch, anything he could get his hands on, and threw them at the attacking birds. Waving his arms and shouting, he drove the birds away.

As the sun was dropping toward the horizon, a great and gloomy darkness settled upon Abram. And he fell into a deep, deep sleep—a sleep like God had given Adam when He took one of Adam's ribs and created Eve.

God spoke again. "Abram, for 400 years, your children will be cruelly treated and suffer many things. They will be slaves in a foreign land." This hardly sounded like good news.

Griffon vultures, with wingspans of more than nine feet, were once common in Palestine. Now they are endangered in some areas. Their gizzard can hold 13 pounds of meat!

But God continued. "I will deliver them. I will punish the nation that enslaves them, and they will leave that land taking great wealth with them." Now, *that* sounded better!

"Abram, you will live to be very old. You will die in peace and will be buried. After your great-great-grandchildren are born, your people will come to this land again." Suddenly fire and smoke flared against the darkness of the night, and Abram saw a smoldering, smoking firepot such as Sarai sometimes used to bake bread. A flaming torch glowed and glinted in the darkness. Floating in the gloom, the fiery pot and torch seemed to "walk" up and down between the butchered animals.

In a flash Abram knew that this was God Himself. It was as though God was saying, "If My

## FROM OUT OF THE STILL AIR CAME A GREAT FLAPPING OF WINGS AND THE HOARSE SCREECHING OF VULTURES.

The ancient technical term for establishing a covenant was "cutting" a covenant. The expression graphically implied that the covenant maker was putting his life on the line.

promises don't come true, then I—God—will be chopped up just like these animals." God was showing Abram that He loved him enough to risk Himself and suffer for him if He did not keep His word. "If I don't keep My word," God was saying, "you can do away with Me and worship some god that the Canaanites worship."

Do you think Abram wanted to worship some make-believe God? Abram had heard the voice of the Creator-God Himself, had seen the fire of His presence, and he trusted Him with all his heart.

<hr />

[1]Genesis 15:1, 2, ICB.
[2]Verses 5-9, ICB.

# Stars and Birds and Firepots

Abram sat sadly in the shade of his tent. He was thinking about God's special promise to him. The Lord had promised a long time ago that he would have a son. But Sarai had never had a baby.

Abram sighed. He was a very rich man, and he had a wonderful wife who loved him very much. He should be content. But, oh, he wanted a baby boy!

That night the Lord appeared to Abram in a vision, a special kind of dream. "I will protect you," God said.

"O Lord, what good are all Your blessings when I don't have a son?" Abram asked. "When I die, my servant will get all my riches."

"No!" the Lord answered. "You will have a son of your very own. When you die, he will inherit all the riches I am giving you."

Then God took Abram outside under the huge night sky. Little insects chirped, and the cool breeze ruffled Abram's beard. "Look up!" the Lord said. "Can you count all the stars?"

Abram tipped his head back and stared at the starry heavens. The more he looked, the more stars he seemed to see. Bright stars, tiny stars, twinkling stars.

"It will be just as impossible to count your children, and your children's children, and all their children as it is to count the stars in the sky," the Lord said, smiling.

Abram believed what God said. And the Lord was very proud of him.

Later, when Abram was 99 years old, the Lord visited him again and said, "I am changing your name to Abraham because Abraham means 'father of many.' And I am changing Sarai's name to Sarah because that means 'princess.' Some of her children's children will be kings."

Abraham smiled. He hugged God's promise in his heart.

—Linda Porter Carlyle

# PLANS AND PROMISES

Sarai cried softly as she lay on her straw mat. Her body shook with muffled sobs, but she buried her head deeper into her blanket, for it would never do to have the servants hear her crying.

She had tried so hard for all these years to ignore the ache for a child of her own. But the hurt just never went away. For years she had clung to God's promise that Abram would have children. Now she was too old to have a baby.

She faced what seemed to be a bitter truth. Abram would have his children as God had said, but not by her. Abram would have to take another wife. In those days many men had more than one wife. In fact, many women signed contracts saying that if they did not give their husband children, he could have children by her slave. Sarai wiped her eyes and stood up. She knew what she must do.

"Girl!" Sarai called. A slim Egyptian girl jumped up from the fire she had been slowly feeding with sticks and fanning to a blaze. Black hair flying, she ran to Sarai. "Yes, Mistress?"

Sarai looked deep into the girl's black eyes. Hagar gazed back, curious, puzzled. Sarai took a deep breath. This was not going to be easy. "You have known," she began, keeping her voice low so that it did not break, "almost since the day that we brought you

out of Egypt of God's promise to my husband. And I think you believe His promise to Abram, the promise of an heir. Am I right?"

Hagar thought fast. It would never do to say that her mistress was wrong. She did worship the God in heaven, but Abram was 85 years old and Sarai just 10 years younger. Carefully she answered, "My mistress is never wrong."

Sarai continued, determined to finish what she had started. "You've been a faithful slave. I've always been able to depend on you. Now I want you to do something for me—and Abram. I want you to help Abram fulfill God's promise. You'll be Abram's second wife so that you might bear him a child."

## SARAI'S IDEA

That night Sarai joined Abram as he strolled around the cluster of tents, checking on his household. In a few words she told Abram her plan. Then she waited for his reaction.

Abram stopped in mid-stride and stared at his wife. In the starlight his eyes seemed to burn right into Sarai's heart. His thoughts jumped and spun like a cornered antelope. After all these years of waiting for God's promise to be fulfilled, was it possible that he had waited for something that would never happen? He believed God's promises, but had God ever said that Sarai would be the mother of his child? Not really! Perhaps he should have taken one of Sarai's servant girls long ago!

As Abram stared at Sarai, he realized that she, no less than he, had waited for God's promise to be kept.

"All right, Sarai," he said with a matter-of-factness he did not feel, "I will take Hagar as a wife to give us the heir God has promised."

The weeks following were long and painful for Sarai. And now as she watched Hagar, there was no mistaking that Hagar's slim body was round with new life. Abram's child was growing within her. And as the child developed within Hagar, bitterness developed

---

**GENESIS 16:1-15**

Sarai . . . had no children. She had a slave girl from Egypt named Hagar. Sarai said to Abram, ". . . [Take my slave girl as your wife.] If she has a child, maybe I can have my own family through her."

Abram did what Sarai said. . . .
When Hagar learned she was pregnant, she began to treat her mistress Sarai badly. Then Sarai said to Abram, "This is your fault. I gave my slave girl to you. And when she became pregnant, she began to treat me badly. Let the Lord decide who is right—you or me."

But Abram said to Sarai, "You are Hagar's mistress. Do anything you want to her." Then Sarai was hard on Hagar, and Hagar ran away.

The angel of the Lord found Hagar beside a spring of water in the desert. . . . The angel said, "Hagar, you are Sarai's slave girl. Where

within Sarai. Why, why should this Egyptian slave bear Abram's child and not she who had been his wife for so many years?

And while Sarai became bitter, Hagar became proud. Her eyes mocked Sarai each time she came out of her tent, which she had moved from the servants' quarters and pitched near Abram's tent. After all, wasn't she carrying Abram's heir?

Sarai vowed to humble her. "Hagar," she instructed, her voice icy, "we need more water from the well." [1]

Hagar turned slowly, her eyes not quite hiding the scorn she now felt for her mistress. "I drew water this morning. You don't really expect me in my condition to get water now, with the sun beating down, do you?" she asked, a new boldness in her voice.

have you come from? Where are you going?"
Hagar answered, "I am running away from my mistress Sarai."
The angel of the Lord said to her, "Go home to your mistress and obey her." The angel . . . also said, "I will give you so many descendants they cannot be counted."

The angel also said to her, "You are now pregnant, and you will have a son. You will name him Ishmael, because the Lord has heard your cries. Ishmael will be like a wild donkey. He will be against everyone. And everyone will be against him. He will attack all his brothers."

The slave girl gave a name to the Lord who spoke to her. . . . "You are 'God who sees me.'" This is because she said to herself, "Have I really seen God who sees me?" . . . Hagar gave birth to a son for Abram. And Abram named him Ishmael. Abram was 86 years old when Hagar gave birth to Ishmael.

# DIAGRAM OF TERAH'S DESCENDANTS

Chart illustrated by Brandon Reese

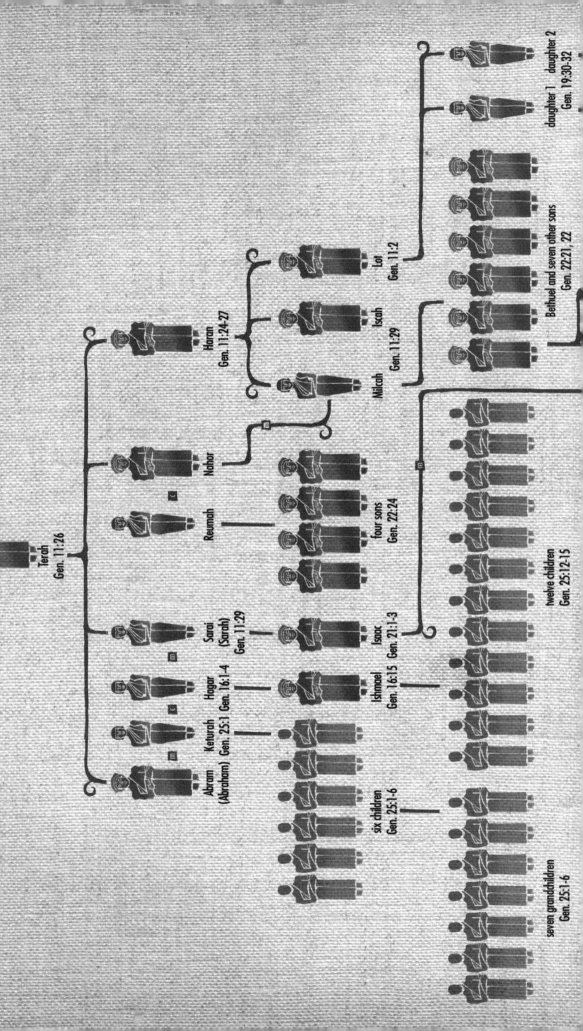

Terah
Gen. 11:26

Abram
(Abraham)

m

Keturah
Gen. 25:1

m

Hagar
Gen. 16:1-4

m

Sarai
(Sarah)
Gen. 11:29

Reumah

Nahor

m

Milcah
Gen. 11:29

Haran
Gen. 11:24-27

Iscah

Lot
Gen. 11:2

six children
Gen. 25:1-6

Ishmael
Gen. 16:15

Isaac
Gen. 21:1-3

four sons
Gen. 22:24

Bethuel and seven other sons
Gen. 22:21, 22

daughter 1   daughter 2
Gen. 19:30-32

seven grandchildren
Gen. 25:1-6

twelve children
Gen. 25:12-15

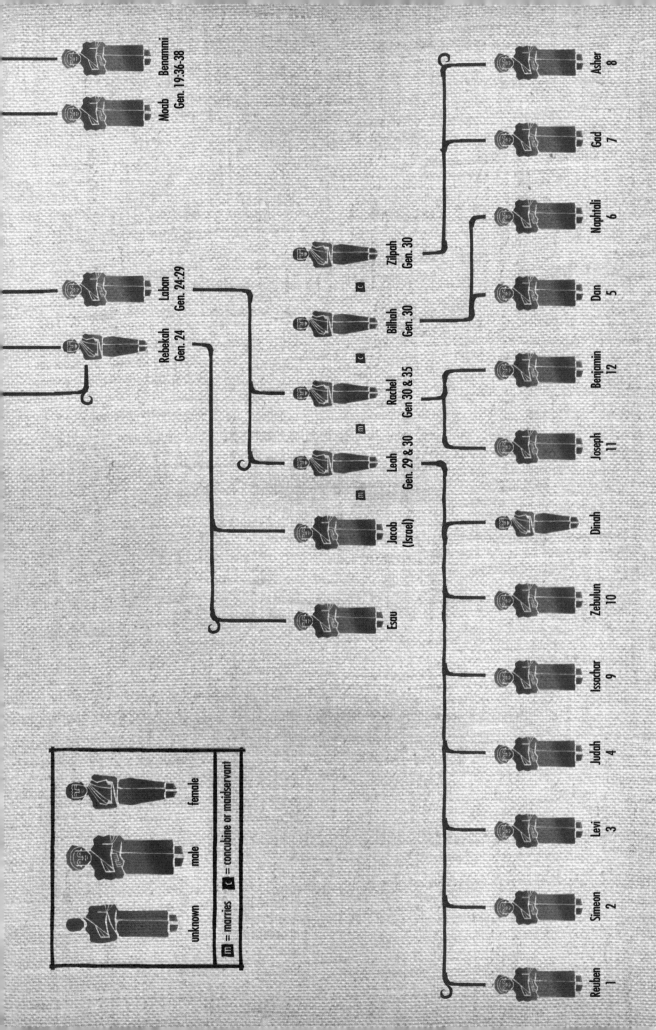

The family of Jacob in Paddan-aram. Gen. 35:23-26 (sons are shown numbered in order of birth)

**Legend:**
- unknown
- male
- female
- m = marries
- c = concubine or maidservant

**Moab** Gen. 19:36-38 — **Benammi**

**Rebekah** Gen. 24 — **Laban** Gen. 24:29

**Jacob (Israel)** m **Leah** Gen. 29 & 30 m **Rachel** Gen 30 & 35

**Bilhah** Gen. 30 (c) — **Zilpah** Gen. 30 (c)

**Esau**

Sons numbered in order of birth:
- Reuben 1
- Simeon 2
- Levi 3
- Judah 4
- Dan 5
- Naphtali 6
- Gad 7
- Asher 8
- Issachar 9
- Zebulun 10
- Joseph 11
- Benjamin 12

**Dinah**

"How dare you speak to me like that?" raged Sarai. "I said to get water!"

"If you insist," Hagar drawled, but she took her time and never brought the water until evening.

"Here's your water," she sputtered, as she spilled some on Sarai's feet.

Before she could think what she was doing, Sarai, strong with anger, slapped Hagar hard, across the mouth.

Hagar's cheeks flamed. "You can hit me all you want, but it still won't make you a mother, will it?" Crying, she ran to her own tent.

Just then Abram stepped from around Sarai's tent. "What's wrong?" he asked.

"What's wrong?" Sarai fumed, half laughing and half crying. "Everything is wrong! This is your fault. I gave my slave girl to you, and when she became pregnant, she began to treat me badly. Let the

Lord decide who is right—you or me."

Abram kept quiet for a moment. He knew Sarai's words were unfair, but he knew she felt deeply hurt. Mixed with his joy at the thought of having a child was an uneasy feeling that perhaps marrying Hagar had not been God's plan after all.

"You're Hagar's mistress. Do anything you want to her," he replied.

"And I *will!*" Sarai promised herself.

## HAGAR RUNS AWAY

That evening Sarai asked Hagar, "Where are the figs I asked you to chop? I see only dates and barley meal here. You really must work faster. And, by the way, I'm having your tent moved back to the servants' quarters. But before you go tonight, I want all those figs chopped."

Hagar looked at the baskets of figs and then at her fingers already red and sore from chopping dates and grinding barley. For once she had nothing to say, but as she cut up the figs late into the night angry tears dropped into the bowl. "I'll show her!" she whispered fiercely.

In the morning Hagar was gone.

Sarai's stomach lurched with a sick feeling of guilt. True, the girl had been impossibly rude, but . . . Then another thought exploded in her brain. The baby! Abram's heir had disappeared with Hagar!

Hagar trudged on as the thin morning light gave way to the blinding beams of the noonday sun. The rocky emptiness shim-

Ishmael lived in Paran. It was high desert that extended from the city of Kadesh-barnea to the granite mountains of the Sinai Peninsula. Today it is known as *et-Tih.*

mered endlessly, but Hagar knew what she was looking for. Soon she would find the spring where all the caravans stopped between Canaan and Egypt.

She paused to drink from the goatskin bag of water she carried with her. Turning it upside down, she let the last drop fall into her up-turned mouth. Hagar licked her dry lips, then walked on. It was farther to the spring than she had thought.

Then in the distance she saw a few oleander bushes marking the location of the spring. There it was—the round stone well. Panting, Hagar leaned against the cool stones of the well and peered into its depth. Water, dark, deep, and inviting, reflected her sweaty face. Hastily she filled her goatskin bag, then gulped greedily as she poured the water into her open mouth and over her hot face. She sank to the ground and pillowed her head against the cool rocks.

The water had soothed her feverish head, and now Hagar began wondering if she'd been foolish to run away. Would anyone in Egypt want a runaway slave?

# HAGAR AND ISHMAEL

God promised Abraham many descendants, but he and Sarah were childless.

Abraham began thinking of ways to bring about God's promise. So he asked God if he could adopt his faithful servant Eliezer, who could then inherit Abraham's estate. The suggestion was not outlandish. Archaeologists have found many cuneiform documents dealing with various permutations of adoption. Most of the adoptions were motivated by the desire for an heir to carry on the family name and estate.

God, however, told Abraham no. "This man shall not be your heir; your own son shall be your heir" (Genesis 15:4, RSV).

Years went by. Abraham and Sarah remained childless. Then Sarah came up with an idea. God had indicated that the promised child would be Abraham's, but He had not mentioned Sarah. Clearly, Abraham needed a concubine. Sarah, who was now in her mid-70s, urged Abraham to take Hagar, her Egyptian slave girl, as a secondary wife. While such a plan may sound strange to us, in the ancient Near

Image of Hammurabi on his law code.

Eastern world this was a legalized way of producing an heir.

Abraham took to the idea. However, from the first the plan backfired. Once Hagar knew she was pregnant, she began treating the barren Sarah with contempt. Sarah sent her packing, but God sent the pregnant Hagar back to Abraham and Sarah. And when Abraham was 86 years old, Hagar gave birth to a boy, whom they named Ishmael. Now Abraham had his own son, and this boy was the heir designate.

When Ishmael was 13 years old, God again addressed the matter of an heir. God promised Abraham a multitude of descendants— but not through Ishmael. Ishmael would indeed have many descendants, but they were not the progeny God had in mind. "I will give you a son by [Sarah]," God said (Genesis 17:16, RSV). The promised "seed" (King James Version language) would be through a son born to both Abraham and Sarah. And sure enough, when Abraham was 100 and Sarah was 90, she gave birth to Isaac.

In an instant the angel of the Lord stood before her and called her by name—something Sarai had avoided doing. "Hagar, Sarai's slave girl, where have you come from? Where are you going?"

Eyes wide with wonder, Hagar answered,

"I am running away from my mistress Sarai."

"Go home to your mistress and obey her. . . . I will give you so many descendants they cannot be counted," the angel said. "You will have a son. You will name him Ishmael. . . . Ishmael will be like a wild donkey. He will be against everyone, and everyone will be against him." [2]

Then the angel disappeared. Hagar talked out loud to herself, hardly believing what had just happened. "Have I really seen God who sees me?" [3]

Hagar, more humble than when she left, returned to Abram's camp and crept back into her tent. And Sarai, relieved to have the future mother of Abram's heir safely home, treated her more kindly.

Fruits commonly eaten in the land of Canaan included grapes, figs, olives, apples, melons, pomegranates, and dates.

Then one day Hagar dropped the yarn she had been feeding onto a wooden spindle. She clutched her stomach. A sharp pain told her that little Ishmael was about to be born.

Sarai helped Hagar into the tent. "I'll send for a midwife," she promised.

Other women gathered around Hagar's tent, waiting for the first cry of the new baby.

Abram stayed out of sight, for having a baby was a woman's business. A big smile spread across his bearded face. Soon he would be a father!

Sarai returned to her own tent and sat, arms hugging her knees and her head down. Bitter tears, held in check for many months, coursed down her cheeks. Abram's heir was about to be born, but not to her.

Suddenly a great shout filled the air as women sang and children jumped and shrieked. "Hagar has had her baby!" they called.

Sarai put on the best smile she could. "I must find Abram," she said to herself as she left her tent. "Abram," she smiled up at him while tears still glistened, "let's go see the heir God has promised."

The other women stood back as Abram and Sarai entered Hagar's tent. Sarai bent to a soft bundle cradled in Hagar's arms. Lifting the tiny baby with its mop of black hair, Sarai placed him in Abram's arms. "Here's your son!" she whispered.

---

[1] The episode of Hagar's rebellion when Sarai told her to fetch water and the time when Sarai had Hagar's tent moved are not in the Bible. Brand has taken the liberty of adding them. They have been added to illustrate what Scripture meant when it records that Hagar "began to treat her mistress Sarai badly" and that "Sarai was hard on Hagar."

[2] Genesis 16:9-12, ICB.

[3] Verse 13, ICB.

# Plans and Promises

*S*arai sat alone in her tent. She was heavy with sadness. She wanted a baby more than anything else in the world! But she was too old to have one.

Sarai had believed God when He promised Abram, her husband, a son. But God had made that promise many years ago. Now Sarai was 75 years old. Women that old do not have babies!

Sarai owned a slave girl named Hagar. Hagar was her property. The law said that if Hagar had a baby, it would belong to Sarai, also. So if Sarai gave Hagar to Abram as a second wife and they had a baby, that baby would be Sarai's. At least lawfully. Sarai sighed and stood up. Maybe it was time to tell Abram about her idea.

Abram listened to his beautiful wife. He loved her very much! He wanted her to be happy. *Maybe,* Abram thought, *this is how God will give me the promised son—by a second wife!* So Abram agreed with Sarai's plan. But he forgot to ask God what *He* thought about it.

Abram took Hagar for his wife. Soon she found that she was going to have a baby. *Ha!* Hagar thought proudly. *I'm going to have a baby, and Sarai can't!* And Hagar no longer wanted to obey Sarai.

Sarai became very, very jealous! She treated Hagar badly. Hagar ran away— far away into the desert. But God found her there, tired and scared. "Go home," God said kindly. "Obey your mistress. You will have a baby boy, and you will name him Ishmael."

Hagar could hardly believe it! God cared about her!

So Hagar did go back home to Abram and Sarai. She did have a baby boy. And she did name him Ishmael, as God had said.

—LINDA PORTER CARLYLE

# VISITORS FROM HEAVEN

Abraham leaned against the tent pole at the opening of his tent, dreaming in the hot sunshine. He was recalling the time God had changed his name.

"*Av-ra-HAHM . . . Av-ra-HAHM . . .*" He said the word slowly, testing it on his tongue and pronouncing each syllable.

"I am changing your name from Abram to Abraham," God had told him. This new name meant "father of a multitude."

And God gave Sarai a new name also. "Her new name will be Sarah," God had said. It meant "princess."

Abraham smiled to himself. Every few years God would visit him and make or remake the same promises.

Suddenly Abraham thought he heard footsteps. He sat up straight. Sure enough, there, a little distance away, stood three strangers. (Back then someone standing a short distance away from one's tent was just the same as a knock at the door!) Quickly Abraham ran to them, bowing as he went.

"Sir," he said to the man who looked like the leader, "if you think well of me, please stay awhile with me, your servant." People in the ancient Near East sounded very polite when they talked to each other. They would heap honor on the other person.

In return, the other person would honor them.

Abraham, ever gracious, continued, "I will bring some water so all of you can wash your feet. You may rest under the tree. I will get some bread for you, so you can regain your strength. Then you may continue your journey."[1]

The strangers flashed happy smiles at Abraham. "Go ahead and do as you have said."

Abraham rushed into the tent and called, "Sarah, Sarah, we have company! Get out 20 quarts of your

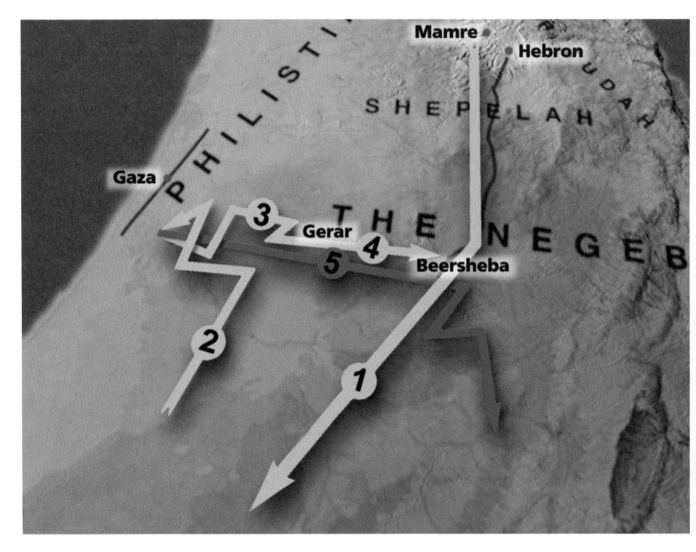

**ABRAHAM'S WANDERINGS IN THE NEGEB**
(1) Abraham left Mamre, following the stream en-Nahar; (2) he pastured his flocks near Shur and then moved north for better fields and water; (3) he spent "many days" at Gerar, where Isaac may have been born; then (4) Abraham moved to Beersheba, where he settled. The red arrow approximates Hagar's flight with Ishmael.

**GENESIS 18:1-32**

Abraham was sitting at the door of his tent. . . . He looked up and saw three men standing near him. . . . He bowed facedown on the ground before them. Abraham said, ". . . Please stay awhile. . . .

I will bring some water so all of you can wash your feet. . . . I will get some bread for you, so you can regain your strength." . . .

Abraham hurried to the tent where Sarah was. He said to her, "Hurry, prepare 20 quarts of fine flour. Make it into loaves of bread." Then Abraham ran to his cattle.

He took one of his best calves and gave it to a servant.

The servant hurried to kill the calf and to prepare it for food. Abraham gave the three men the calf that had been cooked. He also gave them milk curds and milk. . . . Then the men . . . started out toward best flour and make some bread for our guests!" That's a lot of flour. Abraham must have thought that his three guests were very hungry! Of course, it would be shameful to run out of food. Abraham wanted his visitors to have more than enough to eat.

Whirling around to find a servant, Abraham directed, "Quick! Get some water for our guests!" The servant sprang into action. He grabbed the water jug and splashed water from it into basins. Then he ran to the strangers, carrying one basin at a time, the water sloshing on his toes as he ran.

Meanwhile, Abraham had run to the nearby pasture where his cattle grazed. In a pen made of rocks stood a long-eared calf and its mother. Abraham jumped over the stone wall and chased the calf around the pen.

He finally wrapped his long arms around the calf and gave it to a servant to butcher.

"There must be someone special visiting," his servants whispered to one another as they wagged their heads wisely. "Abraham is going to kill the fatted calf, instead of a baby goat."

"Sarah, how is the bread coming?" Abraham asked.

Sarah's eyes twinkled as she rubbed her nose with the back of one flour-coated hand and pointed to the oven. The clay oven shimmered with the heat of the fire burning inside. Abraham flashed her a grateful smile and ran back to help prepare the calf for roasting.

At long last the meal was ready. Abraham invited his three guests to sit on mats under the shade of a big oak tree. They sat cross-legged as they dined. Abraham stood by politely while Sarah, just as politely,

hid behind the tent flap, peeking out and listening.

"This is just a bite to keep you going," Abraham remarked in an offhand way.

He beamed with satisfaction as he watched his guests enjoying the meal. "Won't you have more?" Abraham urged as they began wiping their fingertips clean. "Here, do have some curds with your bread," he urged. The strangers dipped chunks of the freshly baked bread into the tangy white curds.

## WHY SARAH LAUGHED

"Where is your wife Sarah?" they asked.

Sarah, listening behind the tent flap, sucked in her breath. What kind of men were these? How did they know her name? Besides, only people who knew her very, very well would ask such a question! And Sarah had never seen these people before!

"There, in the tent."

Then the leader of the three looked Abraham straight in the eyes, and said firmly, "I will certainly return . . . about this time a year from now. At that time your wife Sarah will have a son."[2]

Sarah gasped, then clapped her hand over her mouth to muffle her sudden laughter. Imagine telling her husband, nearly 100 years old, that his wife, almost 90, would have a baby! She'd been through all that kind of false hope too many times before to believe that now in her old age she would have a baby! Women her age didn't get pregnant. Was this a joke of some sort? A cruel joke at that?

The Stranger continued, "Why did Sarah laugh? Why did she say 'I am too old to have a baby'? Is

Sodom. Abraham walked along. . . .

The Lord said, "I have heard many things against the people of Sodom and Gomorrah." . . .

Abraham asked, "Lord, do you plan to destroy the good persons along with the evil persons? What if there are 50

good people in that city?" . . . The Lord said, "If I find 50 good people in the city of Sodom, I will save the whole city." . . .

Then Abraham said, "Lord, please don't be angry with me. Let me ask you this. If you find only 30 good people in the city, will you destroy it?" The Lord said, "If I

find 30 good people there, I will not destroy the city." . . . Then Abraham said, "Lord, please don't be angry with me. Let me bother you this one last time. What if you find 10 good people there?"

The Lord said, "If I find 10 good people there, I will not destroy it."

In the Hebrew text, Abraham offered the men a little water and a bit of bread. Yet he provided a bounteous and expansive banquet that

anything too hard for the Lord?"

Sarah's face went hot. Her hands turned cold. Hardly knowing what she was doing, she burst out of the tent and boldly lied, "I didn't laugh." She forgot that it was shameful for a woman to talk to strange men.

The Stranger looked at her kindly but seriously. "No. You did laugh."[3]

Sarah turned to the tent, tears blinding her eyes. Shame, hope, excitement, a new trust in God, all

filled her heart. Tears streamed down her face as she remembered the question Is anything too hard for the Lord?

"No, Lord, it isn't," she whispered.

Abraham's guests got up to leave. Still a polite host, Abraham walked with them until they came to a high hill. Far below they could see the Dead Sea sparkling in the sunlight, and the Jordan Valley dotted with its five cities of the plain.

...must have taken his household hours to prepare. Even today Arab sheiks offer generous hospitality to visitors.

Two of the visitors thanked Abraham for his hospitality and continued their journey toward the city of Sodom. The Other stayed behind to talk with him.

The Stranger looked thoughtfully at Abraham, thinking about His next words. "I have another purpose for my visit," he finally said. "The sins of Sodom and Gomorrah shout all the way to heaven. I am here to judge those cities."

Abraham's face turned white. He realized that he was talking to God Himself. Then he thought of his nephew Lot, who now lived in Sodom. Would Lot and his family be destroyed along with the city? And what of other people living in Sodom who worshipped God? Surely there were some!

Stepping close to the heavenly Visitor, Abraham asked, "Do you plan to destroy the good persons along with the evil persons?" Surely the Creator-God was much too fair-minded to do that. Although it would be fair to punish people as wicked as those living in Sodom, it would be terribly unfair to kill good people along with them.

Abraham's forehead wrinkled as he thought about the people in Sodom. He got up his courage and asked, "What if there are 50 good people in that city? Will you still destroy it? . . . Then the good people and the evil people would be treated the same. You are the judge of all the earth. Won't you do what is right?"

The Lord looked into Abraham's troubled eyes and promised, "If I find 50 good people in the city of Sodom, I will save the whole city because of them."

Abraham took a deep breath. But then he began wondering if 50 might be too large a number. "What," he continued, "if there are only 45 good people?"

"If I find 45 good people there, I will not destroy the city."

Abraham did some more math in his head and then asked, "If you find only 40 good people there, will you destroy the city?"

"If I find 40 good people, I will not destroy the city," God assured him gently.

"Lord, please don't be angry with me. Let me ask you this. If you find only 30 good people in the city, will you destroy it?" Would God get angry with Abraham for his boldness?

"No," the Lord answered.

Abraham paused while working the toe of his sandal back and forth in the dust. Did he dare ask for more? After all, he was arguing with God! "I have been brave to speak to the Lord. But what if there are 20 good people?"

Placing a hand on Abraham's shoulder, God agreed that if He found 20 good people, He'd spare the entire city.

Surely, Abraham thought, in the whole city of Sodom there must be 20 righteous people!

---

God considered Abraham to be His friend. So He did not get angry when Abraham reminded Him that He should be fair and not destroy good people along with the wicked.

---

But maybe Abraham was still thinking too big. Let's see. There was Lot, Lot's wife, Lot's two daughters, and their boyfriends. That made six people! Surely there were others—perhaps just four more?

He'd ask God one more question. "Please don't be angry with me. Let me bother you this one last time. What if you find 10 good people there?"

And the Lord assured him, "Yes, Abraham, my friend, for the sake of 10 righteous people I will spare the city."

God then left—and Abraham turned on his heels and headed for his tent.[4]

---

[1]Genesis 18:3, 4, ICB.
[2]Verses 9, 10, ICB.
[3]Verses 13-15, ICB.
[4]See verses 23-33, ICB.

# Visitors From Heaven

The noonday sun warmed Abraham's face as he sat at the door of his tent. Suddenly he noticed three men standing nearby. He got up and ran to meet them. "Come, rest in the shade of my tree!" Abraham exclaimed. "Please stay awhile. My servant will bring some water to wash your dusty feet. And I will fix some food for you to eat."

"OK," the men said.

Abraham rushed to find Sarah. "Hurry! Get your best flour, and bake some bread!" he said.

Abraham helped fix the food. And when it was all ready, he took the warm fresh bread, cheese, milk, and roasted meat to his visitors.

"Where is Sarah, your wife?" the visitors asked as they ate.

"In the tent," Abraham answered. Then one of the men said, "I will come back about this time next year. And when I do, Sarah will have a son."

Sarah was hiding in the tent nearby, and she heard those words. *What a funny thing for a stranger to say to my husband! I'm an old woman. I'm much too old to have a baby!* she thought. And she laughed to herself.

"Why did Sarah laugh?" the man asked Abraham. "Why did she say, 'Can an old woman like me have a baby?' Is anything too hard for the Lord? Sarah will have a son."

"I didn't laugh." she called.

"Yes, you did," the Lord said gently.

Sarah covered her hot cheeks with her hands. Sarah suddenly knew that this was not an ordinary man talking. He knew what she had been thinking. It must be an angel or even God! A son! In a year!

Sarah and Abraham both hugged God's promise in their hearts, and they thought about it every single day.

—LINDA PORTER CARLYLE

# BURNING CITIES

Lot scanned the crowds as they milled around. Here, at the city gate, one could find all kinds of people. Some came crying because a neighbor had stolen their land. Some screamed that a relative had cheated them. Widows demanded the help to which they were entitled. Others came out of curiosity, because exciting things happened at the city gate.

Lot liked being a part of the hustle and bustle of the city. He felt important when people came to him for advice. Lot had become an important man of Sodom.

As he scanned the crowd, he picked out two obvious newcomers. From their dusty feet and clothes he could tell that they had walked far.

Jumping up, Lot ran to the two dusty men, who were really the two angels who had just visited Abraham. But Lot didn't know they were angels. "Please," Lot invited, "come to my humble home and spend the night. It's not much—just a shack, really. But you are most welcome to join us."

"No," they answered, "we will spend the night in the city's public square."[1]

This was the way polite people made arrangements, bantering back and forth, urging one another and deferring to one another. Remember?

Lot pleaded with them to stay with him. "You simply must spend the night with my

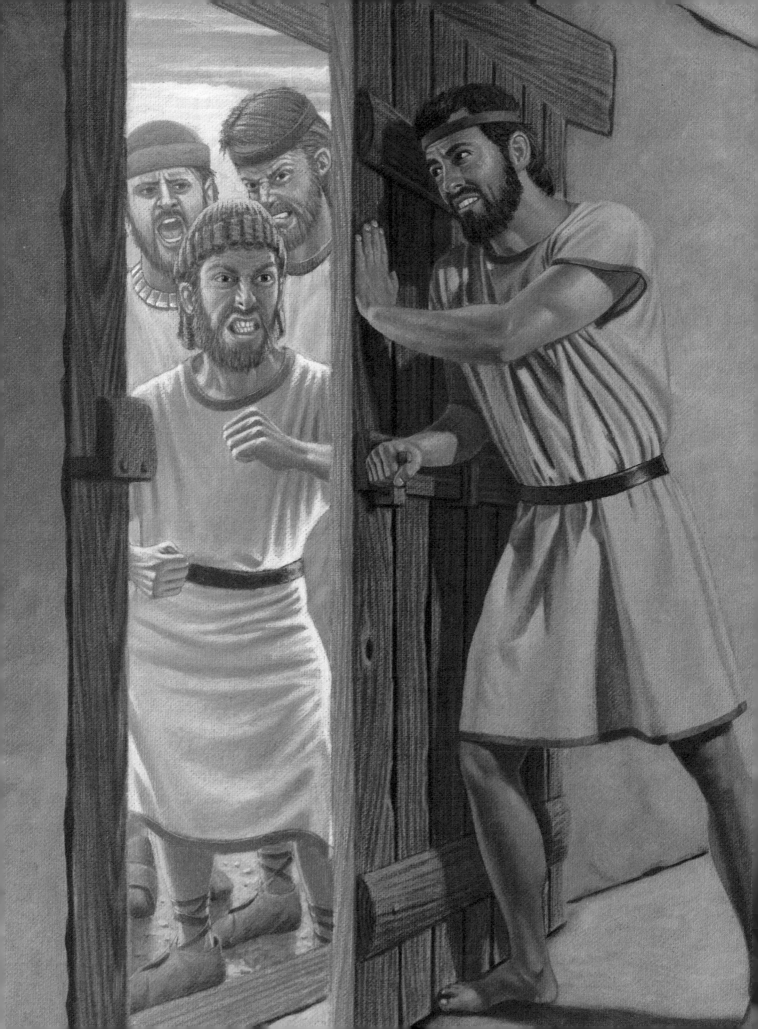

unworthy family. Please show us the honor of spending the night with us."

Finally the angels agreed to go to his comfortable house. When they got inside, Lot offered to wash their tired and dusty feet. He then fed them the evening meal. But unlike Uncle Abraham, who had offered an extravagant meal, Lot fed them crackers.[2]

The strangers quietly ate. They seemed to have something serious on their minds, but they didn't talk about it.

As Lot rolled out mats for his visitors to sleep on, just outside the house coarse, loud voices shattered the stillness. "Hey, Lot!" bellowed a rough voice as someone pounded on the door. "Send out your guests so that we can have a little fun with them!"

## THE RUDE MEN OF SODOM

Scores of men, young, old, rich, poor, surrounded Lot's house. Shouting, swearing, making crude jokes, the mob kept demanding to see Lot's guests.

Lot knew what kind of "fun" these wicked men wanted to have with his guests. Their kind of "fun" would probably leave the two strangers dead by morning.

Lot creaked open the front door and was about to step outside. "Wait! Wait! Let me come out and talk with you," he said. And after having stepped outside, he urged, "No, my brothers! Do not do this evil thing."[3]

The mob shouted more loudly when they saw Lot. "Bring them out!" they yelled.

"Come on, now," Lot begged, truly frightened.

"Look!" he paused in desperation as he saw the sin-crazed eyes of the Sodomites. "I have two daughters. . . . I will give them to you. You may do anything you want with them. But please don't do anything to these men."[4]

Then they shouted to one another, "This man Lot came to our city as a stranger. Now he wants to tell us what to do!"[5] The mob surged forward, about to break down the front door.

"Stand back!" bawled a red-faced brute as he tried to push past Lot. The heavy door creaked and splintered. Desperately Lot tried to squeeze back into the house, but the men were upon him.

Then Lot's guests decided things had gone far enough. With powerful arms they flung open the door and pulled Lot inside. Suddenly the wicked men of Sodom began stumbling around in confusion. They had all become blind! Cursing and moaning, the wicked men, on hands and knees, finally crawled away to their homes.

Lot's eyes grew round with wonder as he stared at his guests. He now understood that these were no ordinary men.

The angels wasted no time now in telling Lot the purpose of their visit. "Do you have any other relatives in this city? . . . If you do, tell them to leave now. We are about to destroy this city."[6]

Immediately the daughters began crying. "What about the men we are going to marry? They have to be warned! Oh, Father, please tell them!"

Lot got up his courage and ventured out into the night. Past altars to Baal he hastened, until he came

---

**GENESIS 19:1-28**

The two angels came to Sodom in the evening. Lot was sitting near the city gate. . . . Lot said, "Sirs, please come to my house and spend the night. . . ."

The angels answered, "No, we will spend

the night in the city's public square."

But Lot begged them to come to his house. So they agreed. . . .

Before bedtime, . . . men . . . surrounded Lot's house. . . . They called to Lot, "Where are the two men who came to you tonight?" . . .

Lot went outside to them. . . .

They started pushing Lot back. They were ready to break down the door.

But the two men staying with Lot opened the door and pulled him back inside the house. . . . The two men struck the men outside the door with blindness. . . .

At dawn the next morning, the angels

The angels had a hard time getting Lot and his family to flee their home in Sodom. It is not easy to leave behind one's belongings.

to the home of a young man who was engaged to one of his daughters. When he saw his future father-in-law, the young man exclaimed with surprise, "What brings you out at this hour?"

Between breaths Lot gasped out the news that Sodom would soon be destroyed. "You must come with us to be saved!"

The young man threw back his head and laughed. "Go back to bed! You'll feel better in the morning!" he scoffed. The young man laughed harder and gently pushed him out the door.

At the next house the other young man opened the door, rubbing sleep from his eyes. "What are you doing here?" he yawned.

Quickly Lot repeated his message, but this young man refused even to let Lot finish speaking. "Do you mean to say you came and woke me up in the middle of the night to tell me a story like that? Sorry, but I'm not in the mood for such nonsense right now. Good night!"

"But—!" The door slammed in Lot's face.

Early the next morning Lot's wife walked around

begged Lot to hurry. They said, "Go! Take your wife and your two daughters with you. Then you will not be destroyed when the city is punished."

But Lot delayed. So the two men took the hands of Lot, his wife and his two daughters. The men led them safely out

of the city. . . . One of the men said, "Run for your lives! Don't look back." . . .

The Lord sent a rain of burning sulfur down from the sky on Sodom and Gomorrah. So the Lord destroyed those cities. He also destroyed the whole Jordan Valley, everyone living in the cities and even all the plants.

At that point Lot's wife looked back. When she did, she became a pillar of salt. Early the next morning, Abraham got up and went to the place where he had stood before the Lord. Abraham looked down toward Sodom and Gomorrah and all the Jordan Valley. He saw smoke rising from the land. It was like smoke from a furnace.

and around her home, fingering her fine dishes, her costly jewelry, her rich draperies and clothes. Lot suddenly felt that all this was somehow unreal. The very reason he had moved to Sodom no longer had meaning. Everything he had would soon be destroyed.

"It's time to go," the angels said.

Lot lingered, but the angels grasped his hand and his wife's and daughters' hands and pulled

---

Lot's wife is unnamed in the Bible, but the rabbis called her 'Idit, 'Irit, or 'Idis. Why the difference in spelling? In Hebrew the letters d (ד) and r (ר) look a lot alike.

---

them from the house. Half dragging them, the angels hurried the little family to the outskirts of the doomed city. "Run for your lives! Don't look back or stop anywhere in the valley. Run to the mountains or you will be destroyed."

"Oh, please, no, not the mountains!" wailed Lot. "I can't run to the mountains. The disaster will catch me, and I will die. Look, that little town over there is not too far away. Let me run there. It's really just a little town. I'll be safe there."[7]

With amazing patience the angels listened to Lot's frantic plea. "Very well, I will allow you to do this also. I will not destroy that town. But run there fast."[8]

Lot and his family headed for the little city. Its name was Zoar, which means "little." Just as they reached it, the sky lit up with a brightness that made the noonday sun look dim. A red glow spread above them, before them, around them. But Lot and his daughters remembered the angel's words, "Don't look back."

Lot's wife stumbled along after her family. Behind her were her home, her fine things, all the little belongings that made life pleasant. She must look one more time at Sodom! Quickly she turned, just for a glimpse, but she never turned around again, because instantly her body became a pillar of salt. Had she been able to see, a fearful sight would have met her astonished eyes. Fire roared through the valley and rained from the sky. The wicked cities of Sodom, Gomorrah, and the other cities in the valley crackled and burned and smoked. Sulfurous gases exploded, and the ever-present tar pits blazed with deadly heat. Burning with the justice of a God who could no longer bear to see people destroy themselves in slow and painful ways, the cities blazed into charred nothingness. Even today no one really knows where the remains of those cities are.

The next morning Abraham hurried to that high hill overlooking the valley, where he and God had talked as they peered down on the cities of the plain. Blackened earth and smoke, dense and billowing, answered his nagging question.

No, there had not been even 10 good people in Sodom.

---

[1]Genesis 19:2, ICB.

[2]The Hebrew word is *matzos*. This is the unsalted cracker that Jewish people still eat at Passover time.

[3]Verse 6, ICB.

[4]Verse 8, ICB.

[5]Verse 9, ICB.

[6]Verse 12, ICB.

[7]Verses 17, 18, ICB.

[8]Verses 21, 22, ICB.

# Burning Cities

Lot sat with the important men in the city gate of Sodom. He saw two strangers coming down the road and stood up to meet them. "Come to my house," he said as he bowed low. "Please be my guests for the night."

The strangers (who were really angels) went home with Lot. And Lot washed their dusty feet and fixed them a meal to eat.

That night the evil men of Sodom surrounded Lot's house. They banged on his door and windows. They shouted, "Bring out those strangers who are in your house!" The bad men of Sodom wanted to hurt them.

Lot stepped outside to talk to the wicked men. "Don't do such a naughty thing," he begged.

The bad men grabbed at Lot to hurt him, too. But the angels opened the door and pulled Lot back inside. Then the angels caused the evil men of Sodom to become blind!

"Do you have any other family here?" the angels asked Lot. "Warn them to get out of this city, because the stink of all its sins has reached God, and He has sent us to destroy it."

Lot ran to warn the men who were going to marry his daughters. But they only laughed at his words.

As morning came, the angels grabbed Lot's hand, and his wife's hand, and his two daughters' hands and pulled them out of the city. "Run for your lives!" the angels shouted. "Don't even look back!"

Then the Lord sent fire, like rain, from heaven, and it burned up the wicked city of Sodom.

Lot's wife hadn't wanted to leave beautiful Sodom at all. She sadly looked back at the city. And she turned into a pillar of salt.

But God kept Lot and his daughters safe from the great destruction.

—LINDA PORTER CARLYLE

# BIRTH OF LAUGHTER,
# BIRTH OF A MIRACLE

Ninety-year-old Sarah moved about the tent with light steps. "Praise be to God," she sang. Standing on tiptoes, she stretched her arms far above her, then threw her head back, and laughed.

Abraham, watching from the door of the tent, laughed too.

"Oh, Abraham! Why didn't you tell me you were there?" cried Sarah, both pleased and embarrassed that he had caught her in such a joyful mood.

Abraham said not a word, but his warm smile showed he felt the same way she did. As he looked at her, he saw God's promise bulging within her, a promise first made to him so many years earlier. Sarah closed her eyes and smiled as she thought of the miracle she carried within her. The scorn of other women, the feeling that somehow she had not deserved the blessing that God had given to them, the ache for a child of her own, all drifted away like a bad dream.

Sarah walked like a princess these days. Head held high, she moved among the servants, observing the new look of respect and admiration in their eyes.

She heard them whispering, and she smiled as she listened to their comments. "Would you ever have thought it? Our mistress is with child! After all these years, and she's 90 years old! It's just a miracle, that's all!"

One servant, however, did not think Sarah's pregnancy was so wonderful. Hagar, dark eyes brooding, shared her thoughts with no one. Her son, Ishmael, would now have a rival!

Sarah noticed Hagar's smoldering silence, but her happiness was too great to let anything disturb it.

Ishmael, a long-legged 14-year-old, had been favored and honored as Abraham's heir. Now he would be forced to take second place. And the baby wasn't even born yet!

## THE PROMISED HEIR

One day as Sarah sang about the tent, her song stopped in midsentence and she caught her breath. At just the time God had promised, Sarah's baby was ready to be born.

"Get the midwife!" she called to a servant. The girl's long legs flew over the ground, and she called to everyone she saw, "The baby is coming. I'm on my way to get the midwife now!"

Word spread quickly, family to family, in all Abraham's vast household. People could still hardly believe it. Sarah, now 90 years old, was giving birth.

Abraham's face turned into one big grin as he wiped his sweaty palms on his tunic. For 25 years he had waited for God to fulfill His promise of a son, a flesh-and-blood heir. Now, today, that promise would become a real, live baby—his son and Sarah's!

Sarah looked up, eyes shining, as the midwife entered her tent. "God has blessed me!" she said with a happy smile.

Buzzing with excitement, the women gathered around Sarah's tent. Abraham was pacing back and forth a little way off. Then with sure, steady hands he selected rocks, as he had done so many times before. Carefully stacking them one on top of another, he built an altar. Later, when his son was born, he would bring a thank offering. Now he knelt before the altar and talked to the Friend who had led him to the land of Canaan so long ago. "Lord," I can hear him saying, "You are the only God. You deliver me from my enemies and forgive me when I sin. You keep Your promises. Today You give me a son, just as You promised! I will teach him to love and obey You so that he can have the same happiness in knowing You that I have!"

Suddenly hundreds of excited voices filled the air. A servant ran across the fields to him, and they met in a cloud of dust. "Your wife . . ." the servant panted, sweat streaming down his face, "your wife . . .!"

"Oh, never mind!" cried Abraham. Forgetting the dignity and honor that ancient Near Eastern men adopted, Abraham gathered his tunic around his waist and sprinted like a boy to Sarah's tent.

> AS SARAH SANG ABOUT THE TENT, HER SONG STOPPED IN MIDSENTENCE AS SHE CAUGHT HER BREATH. HER BABY WAS READY TO BE BORN.

**GENESIS 21:1-8**

The Lord cared for Sarah as he had said. He did for her what he had promised. Sarah became pregnant. And she gave birth to a son for Abraham in his old age. Everything happened at the time God had said it would.

Abraham named his son Isaac. Sarah gave birth to this son of Abraham. Abraham circumcised Isaac when he was eight days old as God had commanded.

Abraham was 100 years old when his son Isaac was born. And Sarah said, "God has made me laugh. Everyone who hears about this will laugh with me. No one thought that I would be able to have Abraham's child. But I have given Abraham a son while he is old."

Isaac grew and became old enough to eat food. At that time Abraham gave a great feast.

In Bible times parents chose names carefully for their newborn children. Personal names held great meaning. Isaac meant "laughter" and signified Abraham and Sarah's joy.

"You may go in," murmured the midwife. With cautious steps and bowed head, Abraham entered the tent. Kneeling by Sarah's mat, he reached out his hand to touch a dear little face. Sarah, face flushed and hair damp with sweat, laughed with joy. Suddenly Abraham laughed too, but his laughter boomed right through the walls of the goat-hair tent. Joy and laughter had come to live with them.

Abraham remembered a time when even he had laughed at God's promises. And Sarah had laughed at God's promise when the angels came to visit them. But now a baby boy, bathed with salt and oil and water and wrapped tightly in a clean blanket, nestled

in Sarah's arms. And Abraham laughed again, out of sheer happiness. "Little Isaac," he said softly, as he lifted the baby from Sarah's arms to his own. "Your name is Isaac, for that means laughter."

"That's a wonderful name, Abraham," Sarah smiled. "It will remind us never to laugh at God's promises. It will also remind us that God has given us reason to laugh with joy in our old age!"

No mother and father ever loved a baby more than Sarah and Abraham loved Isaac. Sarah hardly took her eyes off him, day or night.

"Why don't you let me hold him for a while so you can take a nap?" a servant asked, but Sarah snuggled Baby Isaac closer to her and shook her head. "For 90 years I wondered what to do with my empty arms while other mothers held their babies. Now I have my own baby to hold and love!"

Little Isaac grew and gurgled and smiled. Everyone loved him, for he happily smiled his toothless baby smiles at everyone. His rosy cheeks dimpled and his dark eyes sparkled and he laughed easily. Sarah said to Abraham one day, "He's such a happy baby; I wonder if he knows he's a miracle!"

"I don't think so," Abraham said, a smile lighting his eyes, "but he certainly does live up to his name, for he spreads laughter all around him!"

But Hagar did not laugh. And Ishmael shot hateful glances at the baby who had taken his place.

The years flew by. Little Isaac began to walk. Soon he could say a few words. When he was about 3 years old, Sarah announced, "Isaac is ready to eat grown-up food. He won't need to be nursed any longer!"

"This calls for a celebration!" Abraham exclaimed. "We'll have a party!"

As Abraham had done just a few short years before, he ran to catch the fatted calf. Sarah and her servants slapped flat disks of bread dough onto the outside of the domed clay oven. Other servants set aside goat's milk. Then Sarah said, "We will have a special treat for Isaac. Let's cook grapes and pomegranates until they turn into sweet and tasty syrup!"

As Sarah slowly stirred the fruit over the fire, her face turned bright red and her eyes watered from the heat and smoke, but she kept stirring until brown juice oozed from the fruit and bubbled in the pan. A wonderful aroma drifted in the air, and little Isaac came running. "What's that?" he asked.

*"That,"* smiled Sarah, giving him a hug, "is something good, especially for you!"

Isaac jumped up and down and clapped his hands. But Sarah wasn't through. After letting the syrup, or "honey," as she called it, cool, she mixed it with some bread dough. Into the dough she stirred almonds and raisins, then formed the dough into little cakes and baked them.

"Are those for me?" Isaac asked, all smiles.

"Yes, for you!" Sarah answered.

All Abraham's large household joined the feast. Everyone smiled while watching little Isaac, the miracle child, wrap his chubby hands around the bread and meat and pop it into his mouth. When he drank grape juice from a goatskin bag, everyone clapped and cheered.

"No more baby!" someone called, and everyone laughed. Little Isaac laughed too. Abraham and Sarah laughed. Only two people in Abraham's large household did not laugh: Hagar and Ishmael.

The Bible does not record the conversations surrounding Sarah's pregnancy. Brand has inserted imaginary conversations into the story so that readers can sense some of the excitement that must have blossomed among the members of the household. Such dialogue helps the story become more believable—more real.

# Birth of Laughter, Birth of a Miracle

Sarah and Abraham were old enough to be grandparents. But something amazing had happened. They were finally expecting a baby of their own! Sarah was very excited.

"It will be a boy," Abraham said with a grin.

Everyone was happy—everyone except Ishmael and Hagar. They felt jealous about the new baby who would soon be born.

One day Sarah felt a sudden sharp pain. "Hurry," she told a servant. "Run and get the midwife."

Abraham prayed that God would be with Sarah during this exciting time. And God answered Abraham's prayers by giving 90-year-old Sarah a healthy baby boy.

"We will name him Isaac," Abraham announced, holding the baby close to his heart. "It means 'laughter.'"

"That's a wonderful name," Sarah agreed with a laugh. "God has given us a reason to laugh!"

Sarah and Abraham loved Isaac very much. They smiled as they rocked and fed him.

"Wouldn't you like some help?" a servant asked.

Sarah shook her head. "I love holding and caring for my own dear baby."

Isaac grew to become a handsome boy. He had rosy cheeks and dark eyes. He was such a happy person that everyone smiled when they saw him. "Isaac makes us all laugh with joy," they agreed.

One day Abraham announced, "Tomorrow we will have a party to celebrate that Isaac is growing."

"I will make sweet treats," Sarah said. Isaac especially enjoyed the party. He shared his dessert and smiled at everyone.

"Thank You, God," Abraham prayed that night, "for Isaac, our dear little boy. He is our gift of laughter from You."

—HEATHER GROVET

# BANISHED!

"Some big shot!" Ishmael sneered.[1] "Just look at the new heir, though! Doesn't he look like a 'miracle' with that grape juice running down his chin?"

Ishmael paused to see what impression he was making. Boys about his age gathered around just to see how far he would go in making fun of Isaac, but they didn't dare laugh at either of Abraham's sons.

"Shhh! Here comes Sarah!" one warned.

Ishmael shrugged his shoulders in an I-don't-care attitude, but he wandered off before Sarah reached him.

However, Sarah had seen and heard him—and not for the first time, either. Ishmael's mockery of Isaac had become a part of their lives.

"Isaac," Sarah called. "Come with me while I wash some clothes in the brook."

As Sarah scrubbed clothes in the flowing water and Isaac splashed and played, she thought about Ishmael and Hagar. Always a hot-tempered child, Ishmael had become jealous of Isaac, and his treatment of the younger boy was now nearly unbearable.

Sarah remembered all too clearly that her decision to take the fulfillment of God's promise into her own hands had caused problems from the start. Nevertheless, Ishmael

Isaac, with an eager smile, grabbed the wet cloth in his small, brown hands. As Sarah twisted the other end of the garment, he planted his feet farther apart, and his little face grew red with the effort to hang on to the clothes.

"That's good enough!" she exclaimed when no more water dripped from the robe. "Ready for another?"

While Sarah spread the clean clothes on sun-warmed rocks to dry, she decided that she must ask Abraham to send Hagar and Ishmael away.

That night, from long habit, Abraham and Sarah walked beneath the stars. Sarah's heart beat fast. She remembered as if it were yesterday asking Abraham to take her slave to be the mother of the promised heir. The bitterness and pain of the years since that night seemed to press against her heart, and she could hardly breathe. How would Abraham react when she asked him to send away his firstborn son?

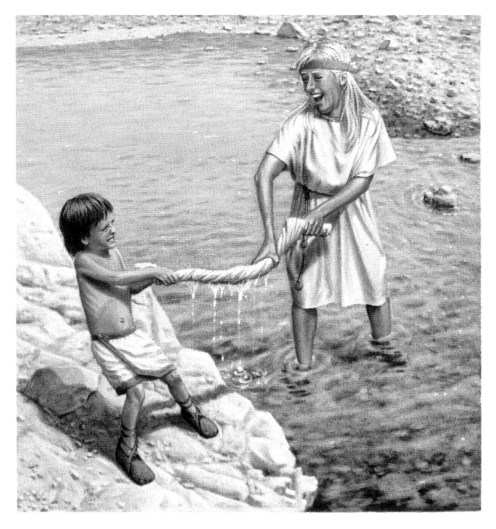

Imagine what it must have been like to do laundry in the ancient Middle East. There were no washers and dryers and no packaged soaps, bleaches, or detergents. All household chores had to be done by hand.

was Abraham's son, and God had promised Ishmael a special blessing also.

Silently Sarah prayed, *"What shall we do, Lord?"*

Sarah lifted a dripping garment from the water. "Here, Isaac, can you hold one end of this tight while I twist?" she asked.

**GENESIS 21:9-21**

But Sarah saw Ishmael making fun of Isaac. (Ishmael was the son of Abraham by Hagar, Sarah's Egyptian slave.) So Sarah said to Abraham, "Throw out this slave woman and her son. When we die, our son Isaac will inherit everything we have. I don't want her son to inherent any of our things."

This troubled Abraham very much because Ishmael was also his son. But God said to Abraham, "Don't be troubled about the boy and the slave woman. Do whatever Sarah tells you. The descendants I promised you will be from Isaac. I will also make the descendants of Ishmael into a great nation. I will do this because he is your son, too."

Early next morning Abraham took some food and a leather bag full of water. He gave them to Hagar and sent her away. Hagar carried these things and her son. She

"Abraham," she began, her voice a little shaky.

"Yes?"

"I have something to ask you, and I know you're not going to like it, but please just listen until I'm finished."

Abraham nodded and looked at her curiously.

"Well, I think we both know now that it was never God's plan for you to have a child by my slave, but how were we to know?"

Abraham nodded again.

"And we both know that Ishmael is not the child of promise. Isaac is," Sarah continued.

"Yes," Abraham agreed, still wondering what Sarah had in mind.

"But Ishmael will not accept second place to Isaac. He teases him and mocks him and makes life miserable for all of us! And Hagar just laughs and lets him do it! It's not right, and I can't stand it any longer!"

Abraham frowned. He'd also noticed Ishmael's mockery of Isaac and his angry moods.

"But what I want to ask you is not just because I want to protect Isaac. You must believe that! I've learned a lot about trusting God since the time the angels visited our tent. When I see Ishmael making fun of Isaac—our living, breathing miracle—I see him making fun of God's promise!"

"What's your point?" asked Abraham.

Sarah looked him straight in the eyes. "Throw out this slave woman and her son. Her son should not inherit anything; my son Isaac should receive it all."

The blood drained from Abraham's face. "I will never part with Ishmael! He's my firstborn son, and although not the promised heir, he is my flesh and blood!"

Late that night as Abraham lay wide-eyed and restless on his mat, God spoke to him. "Don't be troubled about the boy and the slave woman.

### GOD SPOKE TO ABRAHAM. "DON'T BE TROUBLED ABOUT THE BOY AND THE SLAVE WOMAN. DO WHATEVER SARAH TELLS YOU."

Do whatever Sarah tells you. The descendants I promised you will be from Isaac. I will also make the descendants of Ishmael into a great nation. I will do this because he is your son, too." [2]

"Oh, God," he moaned, "this is the hardest thing You've ever asked me to do."

But God had spoken, and Abraham would obey.

In the morning Abraham called Hagar and Ishmael to him. Brokenly he explained that they must leave his household.

Fire flashed from Ishmael's eyes as he listened to his father's words. "It's all because of Isaac!" he cried. "But *I'm* your firstborn! Your inheritance should belong to me!"

Abraham placed his arm around the boy's stiff shoulders. "Oh, Ishmael, it's not your fault that all this is happening. If you would try to be content with a portion of my blessing, if you would treat Isaac

---

went and wandered in the desert of Beersheba.

Later, all the water was gone from the bag. So Hagar put her son under a bush. Then she went away a short distance and sat down. Hagar thought, "My son will die. I cannot watch this happen." She sat there and began to cry. God heard the boy crying. And God's angel called to Hagar from heaven. He said, "What is wrong, Hagar? Don't be afraid! God has heard the boy crying there. Help the boy up. Take him by the hand. I will make his descendants into a great nation."

Then God showed Hagar a well of water. So she went to the well and filled her bag with water. Then she gave the boy a drink.

God was with the boy as he grew up. Ishmael lived in the desert. He learned to shoot with a bow very well. He lived in the Desert of Paran. His mother found a wife for him in Egypt.

more kindly and accept him as my heir—"

"But it isn't fair!" Ishmael spat out the words and turned his back on his father.

Silently Abraham loaded a big goatskin of water and some food onto Hagar's reluctant back. "God will care for you!" he whispered.

Once out of earshot, Hagar turned to Ishmael. "It's not fair, you know! It's not fair!" she cried.

Ishmael's blazing eyes met hers in defiance of God's plan.

But their anger cooled as their steps led them past the fields where Abraham grazed his flocks and into the desert. Hagar remembered another trip into the desert years before when her pride and Sarah's jealousy had driven her to a well where she had met the angel of the Lord. She was sure she could find that well again.

# WHO IS
# THE ANGEL OF YAHWEH?

Genesis 16:7 says: "The angel of [Yahweh] found [Hagar] by a spring of water" (RSV). This is the first time the word "angel" (in English or in Hebrew) is used in the Bible. It is also the first use of the expression "angel of Yahweh."

The Hebrew word translated "angel" is *mal'ak,* which basically means messenger or envoy. The Old Testament uses *mal'ak* for human beings (2 Samuel 3:14) as well as for a supernatural being who represents God to people (Judges 6:12).

Is the angel of Yahweh the same person as Yahweh or different from Yahweh?

In Genesis 16:7 the actor is "the angel of the Lord [Yahweh]." In verse 10 this figure speaks like God Himself: "I will so greatly multiply [Hagar's] descendants that they cannot be numbered" (RSV). Yahweh Himself said similar words to Abram (Genesis 13:16; 15:5). In Genesis 16:11 the angel speaks of Yahweh in the third person—as though Yahweh was a separate being; but verse 13 tells us that it was Yahweh who spoke to Hagar.

So often the distinction between Yahweh and His angel or messenger gets blurred in Scripture that the *Anchor Bible Dictionary* talks about "the apparent interchangeability" of the two and "functional identity" (vol. 1, p. 250). *Harper's Bible Dictionary* observes that the expression "angel of Yahweh" is "almost another designation for God" (p. 30). And the *Holman Bible Dictionary* says that "the distinction between" the angel of Yahweh and Yahweh Himself "is blurred to the point that they seem synonymous" (p. 51).

Because the identity of the individual is distinct, often seeming to be identical with God Himself, some Christian theologians theorize that in most, if not all, cases the angel of Yahweh refers to God the Son before His incarnation through the virgin birth.

This spells Yahweh, God's Hebrew name.

Whatever the case may be—and it is confusing, to say the least—we may conclude that these biblical stories emphasize Yahweh's nearness while at the same time stressing His otherness. Systematic theologians use the term *immanence* when referring to God's self-revealed closeness and *transcendence* when referring to His distance from us. In Scripture the presence of the actor known as the angel of Yahweh indicates that God is ready to perform another wondrous deed for His children.

But the desert stretched on and on. The relentless heat blasted them like a furnace as the sun rose higher and higher in the sky. Their precious supply of water went down, down, even though they tried to drink but little.

Hagar and Ishmael staggered on. They talked little, for the effort was too great. But Hagar's desperate thoughts tumbled in confusion. *What will become of us? How can I find that well? Shall we go to Egypt, or throw ourselves on the mercy of nomads? Or will we die out here in the desert?*

At last the sun dropped below the horizon, and the heat of the day vanished with the sun. Now a cold, damp wind cut through their clothing. Huddled together for warmth and fearful of prowling animals, Hagar and Ishmael spent a sleepless night under the desert stars.

In the morning they ate some bread, washing it down with their last few drops of water. Then they put one determined foot ahead of the other as they faced the empty desert gradually warming from the morning sun.

"Where's the well?" Ishmael demanded.

He swayed as he spoke. His tongue and lips were swollen. His feet hurt.

"It's somewhere near here! We'll come to it soon, I'm sure!" she promised with more assurance than she felt. Still the merciless sun beat down on the homeless wanderers.

At last Hagar spotted a few oleander bushes, and she allowed Ishmael to slump beneath their scant shade.

"My son will die, and I cannot watch this happen," she cried softly to herself. Stumbling to another cluster of bushes, she turned her back on Ishmael. She couldn't bear to watch him die. But she could hear his moans, and she joined her own to his.

Then Hagar heard God's angel's voice. "What is wrong, Hagar? Don't be afraid! God has heard the boy. . . . Help him up. . . . I will make his descendants into a great nation."

Hagar looked up and saw before her the telltale

The biblical text speaks of Ishmael as if he were a toddler at this time. However, he was a teenager—probably 17 years old.

piles of stones marking a well. Crying with relief and joy, she dragged herself to the well. Tears of thankfulness ran down her cheeks as she filled the goatskin bag with water. Running to Ishmael, she wet his lips, his tongue, bathed his face and eyes.

Ishmael would live. God had heard once more, just as he heard Hagar's cry so many years before.

In the years to come, Abraham heard of Ishmael's achievements. His skill with the bow and arrow made him a hunter whose fame spread. When it was time for him to get married, Hagar found a wife for him from her own Egyptian people. And Ishmael became a great nation, just as God had promised.

---

[1]Once again Brand has added some imaginative scenes to flesh out the story.

[2]Genesis 21:11-13, ICB.

# Banished!

Sarah watched Ishmael hold the stick out to little Isaac. Isaac laughed and reached for it. Then Ishmael yanked it away.

Sarah got very angry. Day after day Ishmael teased little Isaac. It had to stop!

"Throw out Hagar and her son!" Sarah shouted to Abraham.

Abraham was very, very sad. He loved Ishmael. But his family was a mess since he and Sarah had decided that he should take a second wife. Abraham didn't know what to do.

God spoke to Abraham. "Do what Sarah wants," God said. God promised to take care of Ishmael and make a great nation of his children.

Early the next morning Abraham gave Hagar some bread and a bottle of water. Hagar cried, and Ishmael shouted in anger. They did not want to leave! Tears ran down Abraham's face, but he sent the two of them away.

Hagar and Ishmael walked and walked in the hot desert sun. They took tiny sips of their water, but soon it was all gone. Their lips dried and became cracked. Their tongues felt like cotton in their mouths.

Finally Hagar told Ishmael to lie down under a little bush. She went a little distance away. Hagar was sure Ishmael was dying. She couldn't bear to watch. She sat down and cried bitterly.

What was that? It was a voice from heaven! "Don't worry, Hagar!" God's voice said. "I will make Ishmael into a great nation." God opened Hagar's eyes, and she saw a well. She ran to it. She filled her water bottle and took it to her thirsty son.

God kept His promise. He blessed Ishmael. Ishmael became a great hunter with bows and arrows. After he got married, he had many sons. Ishmael's children became a great nation, just as God had promised.

—LINDA PORTER CARLYLE

# ABRAHAM'S HARDEST TEST

Cold sweat ran down Abraham's old face, and he sat bolt upright. God's voice, familiar, dear, had spoken to him in the middle of the night, but the words God spoke tormented Abraham like a nightmare.

"Take your only son, Isaac, the son you love. Go the land of Moriah. There kill him and offer him as a whole burnt offering."[1]

Abraham's whole body shivered. Had he heard right? Could this be God speaking to him?

Abraham groaned, "God, what are You asking me to do? Offer Isaac, our reason for laughter, our joy? *You* promised that through Isaac all nations of the earth would be blessed! *You* promised that through him my family would become as numberless as the stars of the sky! And . . . God . . . we *love* him so!"

Abraham could speak no more. Great sobs shook his old body. But his mind kept crying, *Offer Isaac? How can I? How can I?*

God watched Abraham with great love and pity. Did Abraham love God and trust Him enough to offer Him the child he loved most? And if he did, would he understand how much God loves us, even more than fathers and mothers love their boy or girl?

Early the following morning Abraham threw a saddle onto his donkey. His voice was

hoarse with unshed tears as he called the two servants who would travel with them. They came like two shadows in the dim light before daybreak, carrying wood and a firepot with live coals in it.

Finally he went to where Isaac lay sleeping. Just 20 years earlier Isaac had been born. He still seemed little more than a child to his old father.

Isaac's soft breathing stirred his dark curls, and Abraham reached out and gently caressed them. A tear slid down his wrinkled cheek, but he quickly brushed it away.

"Isaac," he called softly.

Isaac opened sleepy eyes. "Yes, Father?"

"Isaac, my boy, come. We must go to the mountains and offer a sacrifice to God."

"Of course, Father!" Isaac agreed. Many times before he had offered sacrifices with his father.

One servant led the frisky donkey. "Stand still!" the servant muttered as the donkey skittered out from under the load of wood and kicked its heels in the air.

Isaac laughed softly at the donkey, but Abraham, usually ready to laugh with his son, only stared at the little gray-brown animal, the crooked pieces of wood, and the smoking firepot.

Off the four men and one donkey headed— toward a place called Mount Moriah, about 50 miles away. And God smiled through His own tears as He noted how much Abraham loved Him.

Abraham passed the next day and the next as if in a dream. His shoulders, already bent with age, drooped lower still under the weight of his burden. Sarah's and Isaac's laughter, usually so welcome to his ears, seemed to echo inside his heart. Could he silence Isaac's laughter? If he did, Sarah's silence would surely follow, for Isaac was her life.

Quick to notice the pain of others, Isaac caught the strange, faraway look on his father's face. "What's wrong?" he whispered.

Abraham placed a hand on Isaac's shoulder and simply shook his head. He didn't trust himself to speak, nor did he know what to answer.

"Lord," Abraham might have whispered, "see me through this. I can't do it alone."

Taking their cue from their master, the servants kept silent also. And Isaac, puzzled by his father's stricken expression and frequent sighs, slowed his pace to match his father's unsteady steps.

The flat plain changed to rocky hills, then a mountain. Abraham, old, grieving, and crushed

**GENESIS 22:1-13**

After these things God tested Abraham's faith. God said to him, "Abraham!"

And he answered, "Here I am."

Then God said, "Take your only son, Isaac, the son you love. Go to the land of Moriah. . . . Offer him as a whole burnt offering. Do this on one of the mountains there. I will tell you which one."

Early in the morning Abraham got up and saddled his donkey. . . . On the third day Abraham looked up and saw the place in the distance. He said to his servants, "Stay here. . . . My son and I will go over there and worship. Then we will come back to you." . . .

Isaac said, "We have the fire and the wood. But where is the lamb . . . ?"

Abraham answered, "God will give us

under the weight of his mission, staggered along the trail, supported by Isaac.

Horrible pictures flashed across Abraham's mind. He saw himself, knife in hand, standing over Isaac's young body. Then he saw that body lying lifeless and bleeding on an altar. His mind screamed, *No!*

In his imagination Abraham could see Isaac, his eyes dark with horror and fear, staring at him. *"I'm* the sacrifice? Are you sure?"

And he could see Isaac, shaking with terror, back away from his father shouting, "Don't come near me! Don't!" as with a last look of shock and loathing, he bolted from the mountaintop. He could see himself alone, despised by his son and forsaken by God.

Abraham groaned; the pictures inside his head seemed so real! With effort he pushed the terrible scenes from his mind and thought about God and His promises. He remembered the time God delivered Sarah from Pharaoh. He thought about the heathen kings whose armies God had stopped from attacking his household. He pictured again the wonderful vision God had given him, and he heard God's voice saying sweetly, surely, "Your children will number more than the stars of the sky or the dust of the ground. And Isaac is the promised child."

I can see Abraham's faltering steps grow stronger as God fills his mind. His promises wrapped around Abraham like loving arms.

Abraham breathed, "God, You brought Isaac to us from Sarah's old body when no new life could grow there. If You can do that, You can bring Isaac back to us from the dead, for I know

Wells sometimes were within city walls and sometimes outside city walls. They were always very valuable. Sanitary drinking water was always problematic.

You, my God, and You keep Your promises!"

Not far from the base of the mountain, Abraham turned to his servants. "Please wait here for us. My son and I will go worship, then return to you."

Silently Abraham shifted the wood from the donkey's back to Isaac's. Abraham next picked up the knife and the firepot.

Isaac could no longer hold back his questions. "Father," he asked gently, cautiously, "we have here the wood and the live coals for the fire, but where is the lamb for the burnt offering?"

Abraham could hardly speak past the lump in his aching throat. "The Lord will provide the sheep."

the lamb for the sacrifice, my son." So Abraham and his son went on together. They came to the place God had told him about. There, Abraham built an altar. He laid the wood on it. Then he tied up his son Isaac. And he laid Isaac on the wood on the altar. Then Abraham took

his knife and was about to kill his son.

But the angel of the Lord called to him from heaven. The angel said, "Abraham! Abraham!"

Abraham answered, "Yes." The angel said, "Don't kill your son or hurt him in any way. Now I can see that you respect

God. I see that you have not kept your son, your only son, from me."

Then Abraham looked up and saw a male sheep. Its horns were caught in a bush. . . . [Abraham] offered it as a whole burnt offering to God. Abraham's son was saved.

At the top of the mountain Isaac swung the wood off his shoulders and helped his father gather some of the rocks strewn about the ground. Abraham's hands shook as he picked up one, then another. Slowly, carefully, father and son placed the rocks on top of each other to form an altar.

With one last silent cry for courage, Abraham threw his arms around his son, and sobbed out the dreadful secret of the missing sacrifice.

The color drained from Isaac's sun-tanned cheeks, but he made no move to run away. Holding his father

In Ur, Abraham's birthplace, archaeologist Sir Charles Leonard Woolley found two statues of a male sheep or goat caught in a bush. It is constructed from gold, lapis lazuli, and shell.

© Copyright The British Museum

close, he whispered, "We will do what God commands! Here, let me help you!"

The rope to bind the sacrifice trembled in Abraham's hands as he tied it around Isaac. Abraham piled the wood on the altar, and Isaac, guided by his father's hands, stretched himself upon it.

The altar, the wood, the sacrifice, awaited only a gleaming knife and hungry flames. Abraham's eyes, like coals themselves, burned into Isaac's.

In anguish Abraham readied the knife to plunge it into the body of his beloved son.

*"Abraham! Abraham!"* Abraham felt his arm seized in an iron grip, and the knife slid from his

hand and clattered onto the rocky ground.

Joyfully, fearfully, hopefully, he answered. "Yes! Here I am!"

"Don't do a thing to hurt the boy," God's voice, full of love, commanded. "You have passed the test, Abraham. You have proved that you love Me so much that you would do anything for Me; you would even give Me Isaac, the son of promise."

Suddenly Abraham saw a ram, struggling to free its horns from some bushes. "My son," Abraham spoke brokenly, thankfully, "over there is our sacrifice!"

Together father and son worshipped. As the fire and smoke of their burnt offering drifted toward heaven, they praised the God who always keeps His promises, the God who provided the ram for their offering.

"I will call this place 'The Lord Gives!'" exclaimed Abraham.[2]

Then, once more, Abraham heard God's voice. "I make you this promise by my own name: I will surely bless you and give you many descendants. They will be as many as the stars in the sky and the sand on the seashore. . . . Through your descendants all the nations on the earth will be blessed. This is because you obeyed me."[3]

Arms wrapped around each other, and faces shining, Abraham and Isaac scrambled down the mountain, rejoined the servants, and returned home.

---

[1] Genesis 22:2, ICB.
[2] Verse 13, ICB.
[3] Verses 16-18, ICB.

# Abraham's Hardest Test

"Abraham!" It was God's voice speaking.

"Here I am," Abraham answered.

"Take Isaac to Mount Moriah. I want you to sacrifice him as an offering to Me."

How could God ask such a thing? Worshippers of false gods, not worshippers of the true God, offered human sacrifices. Besides, God had given him Isaac after years and years and years of waiting for a son. God knew that Abraham loved Isaac more than anything else in the world. Oh! Could that be it? Was God really asking him if he loved Isaac even more than he loved God?

Abraham had never felt so sad in all his life. But he knew that as much as he loved Isaac, he did not love him more than he loved God.

Early the next morning Abraham cut some wood for the sacrifice. He loaded up his donkey. "Come with me," he said to Isaac. "We are going to make a sacrifice to the Lord."

Abraham, Isaac, and two servants walked and walked. It was a long trip to Mount Moriah.

As Abraham and Isaac climbed toward the top of the mountain, Isaac said, "Father, I see you've brought wood and coals, but where is the lamb?"

Abraham took a deep breath. "God will provide," he answered.

When they reached the top, Abraham and Isaac built an altar. Abraham carefully arranged the wood on it. Then, with tears in his eyes, he told Isaac what God had asked him to do.

Isaac hugged his father a long time. Then he lay down on the altar.

"Abraham!" God's voice called. "Stop! Now I know how much you love Me!"

Abraham's heart filled with joy! When he looked around, he saw a ram caught in a bush. The Lord had provided a sacrifice!

"I will richly bless you," God's voice said, "because you obeyed Me."

—LINDA PORTER CARLYLE

# UR TODAY

The background photo shows part of the marshlands in Iraq that once spanned more than 7,000 square miles between the Tigris and Euphrates rivers. This region was not far from ancient Ur, where Abraham was born. Some scholars speculate that this area was where the Garden of Eden was located. Porcupines, otters, soft-shelled turtles, carp, shrimp, ibis, warblers, babblers, darters, and thousands of other wildlife thrive here. Between 1990 and 1994 Saddam Hussein drained some 60 percent of this ecosystem.

The Ma'dan people, who live in this area, construct islands and houses from the reeds that thrive here.

The houses made of mud and reeds are called *mudhif* or *sarifa's*. Today's dwellings closely resemble those constructed 5,000 years ago by their Sumerian and Babylonian ancestors.

Water buffalo provide milk, butter, and hides. The children use them as diving platforms.

Some 300,000 of the 500,000 Ma'dan people who live here had to flee their settlements because of Hussein's draining of the marsh-lands, which has been called "one of human-ity's worst engineered disasters." Parts of this bionetwork are now being reflooded.

Sir Charles Leonard Wooley found this lyre in the grave of Queen Pu-Abi (ca. 2600 to 2500 B.C.) in Ur. The skeleton of a woman lay next to this musical instrument, with her hands placed on the strings.

The background photo is of the partially rebuilt ziggurat that was originally built by King Ur-Nammu to the moon god named Sin. This ziggurat was constructed between 2113 and 2096 B.C. Ziggurats were stepped temple-towers. They were erected around mounds of clay and reeds and typically had from three to seven levels. Remains of around 25 ziggurats still exist. The best preserved is this one built by Ur-Nammu at the city of Ur, Abraham's birthplace.

Also found in the royal cemetery were several game boards now called the "Game of Ur." It is said that this was one of the most popular games in the ancient Near East. The board itself was wood with inlays of shell, red limestone, and lapis lazuli. By throwing dice, two players competed in trying to get a game piece from one end of the board to the other.

This necklace or headdress made from gold, lapis lazuli, and carnelian was found in Queen Pu-Abi's grave. The blue lapis luzuli was imported from Afghanistan. Twenty-five attendants (and some oxen hitched to carts) were buried with her in her tomb.

# BIBLE GLOSSARY/DICTIONARY

Here is a list of the biblical people and places mentioned in this book. The glossary not only gives information about each person and place, but also provides two guides that use easy-to-understand pronunciation apparatus. When a syllable is given in all capital letters, that is the syllable you put the stress on.

The first pronunciation offered is how most people who speak American English say the name. The second pronunciation is truly special. It tells you how to pronounce the name in Hebrew, Egyptian, Persian, Babylonian, Aramaic, or Greek. We give special thanks to Leona G. Running, expert in ancient Near Eastern languages, for preparing the pronunciation guides.

Have fun reading about these fascinating people and places of long ago. And enjoy the edge you'll have when it comes to biblical trivia, because you will be able to pronounce those tongue-twisting names just as they were spoken in the ancient Near East.

**ABRAM**—*American English pronunciation: AY-bram. Hebrew pronunciation: av-RAHM.* The name means "exalted father." Terah originally called his son Abram, not Abraham, which was a new name that God gave Abram after he was living in Canaan.

**ABRAHAM**—*American English pronunciation: AY-bra-ham. Hebrew pronunciation: av-ra-HAHM.* The name Abraham means "father of a multitude." Born in the city of Ur, he lived in the city of Haran until his father, Terah, died. Then God told him to leave for an unknown land— the "prom-

Abraham

ised land"—Canaan. He left the urban lifestyle of Haran when he was 75 years old for a nomadic way of life. God covenanted with Abraham, promising to give him land and descendants and making him a blessing to the world. When Abraham was 100 years old, Isaac was born. Abraham died at 175 years of age. Scripture refers to him as a friend of God (2 Chronicles 20:7; cf. Isaiah 41:8). Scholars differ as to when he lived. Some think he lived during the Early Bronze Age (3000-2000 B.C.). Others believe he lived during the Middle Bronze Age (2000-1500 B.C.). Constance Gane, who has provided information for our timelines, locates him toward the end of the Early Bronze Age. Abraham is an important figure for Judaism, Christianity, and Islam.

**ANCIENT NEAR EAST—** (Not in the Bible.) The Near East is typically a synonym for the Middle East—the area covering southwest Asia and northeast Africa. Palestine was part of the Near East.

**BABYLON—***American English pronunciation: BAB-ill-on. Hebrew pronunciation:*

Babylon

*bah-VEL. Babylonian pronunciation: bahb-EEL-ee.* This is the name of a famous ancient Mesopotamian empire that began with its capital city at Isin, later at Ur (see below), and even later yet at the city of Babylon. It was situated in the southern part of Mesopotamia (see below). The land of the Babylonian empire had little in the line of natural resources such as stone, metals, and trees for lumber. Buildings were constructed from mud bricks. In 2017 B.C. an Amorite king named Ishbi-Erra founded

what archaeologists refer to as the first dynasty of the Early Old Babylonian Empire. He insisted that his people refer to him as "Ishbi-Erra-Is-the-God-of-His-Land" or "Ishbi-Erra-Is-My-God" (among other titles). He died in 1985 B.C. The time between 1792 and 1750 B.C. is often referred to as the Hammurabi Age. King Hammurabi was the sixth king in the first dynasty of Babylon. He was very interested in maintaining law and order and published a law code. He also promulgated *mesharum*, orally

Bethel still exists as modern Beitin.

transmitted examples of how justice should be maintained. From 1750 to 1595 B.C. the Babylonian Empire started to fall apart. It was not until 626 B.C. that the Neo-Babylonian Empire was constituted under King Nabopolassar, a Chaldean chieftain and father of King Nebuchadnezzar, who is mentioned in the Old Testament.

**BETHEL**—*American English pronunciation: BETH-el. Hebrew pronunciation: bayth-AIL.* The city of Bethel, originally called Luz, was an important religious center in Canaan and is 11 miles north of Jerusalem. The name means "house of God." (There was even a northwest Semitic god by the name of Bethel, who was supposed to be one of the sons of Heaven and Earth. Some evidence points to the possibility that the word also referred to stones that were superstitiously regarded as being alive.) Archaeological evidence points to inhabitants in the area as far back as possibly 3200 B.C., but the city itself was probably founded around 2000 B.C. The city is close to the town of Ai. Other than the city of Jerusalem, Bethel is the place most often mentioned in the Old Testament. At one point in its history, the city had walls that were 11 feet thick. Abraham in his wanderings in Canaan lived there on at least two occasions. It is where Jacob later had a dream about God's presence while he was fleeing home (and his brother Esau) on the way to Uncle Laban's place in Mesopotamia. During the time of the judges the ark of the covenant was housed at Bethel. For a while the Hebrew sanctuary with the ark of the covenant was situated in Bethel. The prophet Samuel performed some of his administrative duties here, and during the time of Elijah a school of the prophets was located here. Bethel still exists as modern Beitin.

**CANAAN/CANAANITES**—*American English pronunciation: KAY-nan. Hebrew pronunciation: ke-NA-an.* Canaan is the equivalent of Palestine—the area between the Mediterranean Sea and the Jordan River. The people who lived here were called

Canaanites and were descendants of Ham's son, Noah's grandson, by the same name. Canaan was first referred to in written documents around 2300 B.C., but archaeologists say that they have uncovered evidence of civilization there dating back to 3000 B.C. The Canaanite city known as Ugarit had a library (perhaps for priests), which archaeologists have discovered. The language of Canaan was absorbed by Abraham's descendants, becoming the language now known as biblical Hebrew.

**DAMASCUS**—*American English pronunciation: da-MASS-kus. Hebrew pronunciation: dam-MESS-ek.* The city of Damascus is arguably the world's oldest continuously inhabited city and still exists—as the capital of modern Syria. According to the Jewish historian Josephus, the city was founded by one of Shem's grandsons. It was the capital of ancient Aram from the tenth to the eighth centuries B.C. The city is situated on the banks of the Barada River (ancient Abana River) and on a plateau some 2,200 feet above sea level.

The city itself forms part of the oasis of Ghuta, which is pretty much on the edge of the desert. In ancient times its patron deity was Hadad, a storm and fertility god. The city was famous for its gardens and orchards, and its wine was well known throughout the ancient Near East. The fabric that today we call "damask" comes from the name of this city, where this special cloth originated.

**DEAD SEA or SEA OF SALT in Hebrew**—*American English pronunciation: DEDD SEE. Hebrew pronunciation: yahm ham-MEH-lakh.* Also called the Salt Sea, Sea of the Arabah, Sea of the Plain, and the Eastern Sea. It is the biggest lake in Palestine (nearly 50 miles long and 6 to 10 miles wide) and the lowest body of water anywhere on earth—1,320 feet below sea level. Each day the Dead Sea takes in more than 6 million tons of water from the Jordan River (other rivers and streams also flow into it), but the lake has no outlet. The area gets an average of 330 full days of sunshine annually, so evaporation makes the water very dense with 21 mineral salts. Its salinity is 25 to 28 percent,

Dead Sea shoreline

TODD BOLEN/BIBLEPLACES.COM

in contrast with 4 to 6 percent salinity of ocean water, making it the saltiest body of water in the world. At the bottom and around the edges of the Dead Sea, salt precipitates out and piles up. Only a few fish can live in it, but only near its inlets. Anyone can easily float in the Dead Sea, and when swimmers leave the lake, their bodies are coated with salt. From 1947 to 1956 more than 800 scrolls were found in nearby caves. These scrolls come from an area known as Qumran, the location of a group of Essenes, an ascetic cult of Judaism. There are biblical and nonbiblical scrolls in the findings. They are written in Hebrew or Aramaic and were hidden sometime between A.D. 66 and 70. The biblical Dead Sea scrolls (usually abbreviated DSS) are the oldest biblical manuscripts available to scholars. Some contain psalms of David that were not preserved in the Judeo-Christian Bible. The DSS have given biblical scholars many insights into the culture and language of turn-of-the-era Judaism.

**EBAL**—*American English pronunciation: EE-bal. Hebrew pronunciation: ay-BAHL.* At 3,109 feet above sea level, Mount Ebal is one of the tallest mountains in Palestine. It is separated from Mount Gerizim by a small valley. Mount Ebal is steep and rocky, with little vegetation. From this mountain Moses had the curses that would plague those who broke covenant with Yahweh read to the Israelites. Joshua also was to erect an altar and some memorial stones there. Ebal is just north of the city of Shechem. In 1980 archaeologists uncovered a religious site there— probably a shrine or temple of

some sort. A large altar discovered at Ebal was built probably around 1200 B.C.

**EDEN**—*American English pronunciation: EE-den. Hebrew pronunciation: AY-den.* The Hebrew place name Eden probably means either "steppe" or "delight." It was the name of the plain on which God planted a luxurious garden for Adam and Eve to live in. According to Genesis, two special trees grew in Eden. One was the tree of life; the other was the tree of the knowledge of good and evil. God gave

Eden

Adam and Eve only one commandment (not 10): Do not eat the fruit growing on the tree of the knowledge of good and evil. They did, thus rebelling against God. Much speculation has gone into identifying Eden and its garden. No one knows for sure where it was situated, although some scholars think it was somewhere in Mesopotamia. Much later in the Old Testament the Garden of Eden seems to be identical with the Garden of God.

**EGYPT**—*American English pronunciation: EE-jipt. Hebrew pronunciation: mits-RAH-yim.* The present English word "Egypt" comes from the Greek. In the Old Testament Egypt was known as Misrayim. This northeastern African country was divided into Lower Egypt (the Nile Delta, also known as the "Black Land") and Upper Egypt (the Nile River Valley, also known as the "Red Land"), and the Hebrew ending *ayim* is a dual ending, probably referring to this distinction. Although technically part of the Sahara Desert, Egypt has been a fertile land because of the Nile River, which overflows its banks each year, bringing irrigation and rich mud in the Nile River

Egypt

delta. Wheat, barley, flax, and grapes have been the main crops for thousands of years. Also, in areas date palms, fig trees, acacias, and sycamores thrive, but Egypt has never had any forests. In the swampy areas, papyrus grew in abundance, and the Egyptians used the plant to make what eventually came to be known as paper. Egypt also has had some interesting wild animals living in its territory—Nile crocodiles, hippopotamuses, hyenas, and jackals. The people who lived in ancient Egypt were Hamitic, not Semitic—descendants of

Noah's son Ham. The earliest Egyptians appear to have been slight of stature with swarthy complexions and black hair. These farmers expanded their horizons, and ultimately Egypt became one of the great nations of the ancient world. The Egyptian kings were known as "pharaohs." The Egyptians worshipped many gods and became especially concerned about the journey to a better land for those who died. As a result, much effort was expended in building elaborate graves—especially the pyramids. Abraham took refuge there during a famine in Canaan. Joseph ended up in Egypt as a slave and later as second to the pharaoh himself. Joseph moved his entire family to Egypt, where they lived for many years. Moses was born in Egypt years later and ultimately led the Israelites in the exodus from Egypt to the Promised Land.

**ELIEZER**—*American English pronunciation: el-ee-EE-zer. Hebrew pronunciation: el-ee-EH-zer.* The name Eliezer means "my God is a helper." The Bible mentions 11 different men with this name. The Eliezer referred to in this book was Abraham's servant, apparently born in Abraham's own household but with ancestors from Damascus. If Abraham had not had any sons, by ancient custom Eliezer would have become his heir. Abraham sent Eliezer to Haran to find a wife for Isaac—Rebekah.

**ENOCH**—*American English pronunciation: EE-nok. Hebrew pronunciation: ha-NOHK.* Two men and one city in the Old Testament bore the name Enoch, which means "dedicated one." His father was a man called Jared, and the

Enoch and Methuselah

RAOUL VITALE

Bible says that Enoch was the "seventh from Adam." He is said to have "walked with God" after his wife gave birth to Methuselah. Scholars are not sure how to understand the Hebrew behind the expression "walked with God," because it has the definite article and uses the plural form of God, which can be translated "walked with the gods" (in the Hebrew Bible, angels were sometimes designated by the Hebrew word *elohim*, God or gods). When Enoch was 365 years old, God translated him—took him alive

to heaven without dying.

**GERIZIM**—*American English pronunciation: GAIR-eh-zim. Hebrew pronunciation: ge-riz-EEM.* Mount Gerizim, which actually has three summits, was paired with Mount Ebal when Moses told the Israelites that after entering Canaan they should gather at these two mountains and have the curses and blessings read to them. The blessings were read from Mount Gerizim, which is south of the city of Shechem. The mountaintop is 2,891 feet above sea level. Archaeologists have discovered a temple here that dates back to the Middle Bronze Age (2000-1500 B.C.) Today it is called *Jebel et-Tor*. Judges 9:37 calls Gerizim the "center of the land" (ICB), which probably means it was considered to be the navel of the world—a place where heaven and earth touch or intersect. Modern Samaritans still hold their sacred annual feasts on Mount Gerizim.

**GOMORRAH**—*American English pronunciation: go-MORE-ah. Hebrew pronunciation: a-moh-RAH.* Gomorrah (the meaning of its name is unclear) and its sister city Sodom were situated in the Jordan River valley not far from the Dead Sea. All told, there were five "cities of the valley" (or plain). Because of their wickedness, God destroyed these cities. Archaeologists are not sure of the location of ancient Gomorrah. Some people think that it may be under the waters of the Dead Sea. Others speculate that it was situated elsewhere. For example, some think the twin cities of Gomorrah and Sodom were at the northern end of the Dead Sea, by the mouth of the Jordan River. Others are convinced that they were at the south end of the Dead Sea.

**HAGAR**—*American English pronunciation: HAY-gar. Hebrew pronunciation: hah-GAHR.* Hagar was Sarah's Egyptian maidservant. She was probably just a young girl when Sarah acquired her—perhaps when Abraham and Sarah had fled to Egypt during a famine in Canaan. The name was common in ancient Arabia and later also referred to a country and its people. When Sarah was old and had not yet given birth to the promised son, she told 85-year-old Abraham to take Hagar as a wife so that a son could be born to Abraham, if not to both Abraham and Sarah. Hagar became pregnant and began acting rebelliously with Sarah. She was expelled from the camp twice, the first time before she gave birth to Ishmael and the last time when Ishmael was probably in his midteens.

**HARAN**—*American English pronunciation: HAY-ran. Hebrew pronunciation:*

Hagar

Hebron

*bah-RAHN.* Although in English this personal name is spelled like the city's name (see below), in Hebrew the initial letter is different. Three different people in the Old Testament had this name. The Haran in this book was Abram's brother. He died in Ur before Terah moved his family to the city of Haran, leaving one son, Lot, and two daughters, Milcah and Iscah, without a father.

**HARAN**—*American English pronunciation: HAY-ran.*

*Hebrew pronunciation: bah-RAHN.* Haran was a very old city in northern Mesopotamia and appears to have been founded in the mid-third millennium B.C. The root behind the name probably meant something like "road," "crossroads," or even "business trip." Haran was an important religious and political center early on. It and the ancient city of Ur, which was in southern Mesopotamia, were centers of worship of the moon god Sin. According to one chronology, about the time that Terah and his family left ancient

Ur and moved to Haran the Elamites had destroyed Ur. In fact, that may have been the reason Terah took the long trip north from Ur to Haran, where Terah died. After Terah's death, when Abram was 75 years old, Abram and his immediate family left Haran for the Promised Land. Later Isaac and Rebekah sent Jacob to Haran to find refuge from his angry brother Esau. There Jacob lived with Uncle Laban and married his cousins Rachel and Leah. Many hundreds of years later Haran was the last capital of the Assyrian Empire. Nabonidus, the last native Babylonian king, reconstructed the temple to Sin in Haran and made his mother its high priest.

**HEBRON**—*American English pronunciation: HEE-bron. Hebrew pronunciation: hev-ROHN.* This word can refer to both a place and a person. In this book it is used only of the place. Hebron was an important city in the hill country, with an altitude of 3,350 feet above sea level. It is located about 20 miles from Jerusalem and was originally known as Kiriath-arba. The city was situated on some major trade routes. The ancient site is today known as *Jebel er-Rumeidah.* Abraham lived in the vicinity of Hebron for some time, and here he bought the Cave of Machpelah, where he, Sarah, Isaac, Rebekah, Jacob, and Leah were buried. Some have pointed out that this was the first Jewish purchase of real estate in Israel. Nearly 2,000 years later Herod the Great constructed an enclosure around the burial site, and parts of the wall still stand inside the church (built during the Byzantine Period) that now marks the spot. There is

a modern city called Hebron that is situated nearby the ancient site. Modern Hebron is sometimes called *el-Khalil,* which in Arabic means "the friend," a takeoff on Abraham's title in Scripture, "Friend of God."

**ISAAC—***American English pronunciation: EYE-zak. Hebrew pronunciation: yits-HAHKH.* The name Isaac means "he laughs." He was the son of Abraham and Sarah, the child God promised through whom the whole world would be blessed. Because of

Sarah's barrenness, they had just about given up on the idea they would have a child. Sarah's pregnancy was considered miraculous and a direct result of God's promises to them. Abraham was 100 years old and Sarah 90 when Isaac was born. They had entered Canaan 25 years before Isaac's birth. Isaac married Rebekah, and they had two sons—Jacob and Esau. For a while Isaac lived at a place called Gerar, where God renewed with Isaac the covenant He had originally made with Abraham. From Gerar Isaac moved to Beersheba. He was 180 years old when he died.

**ISHMAEL—***American English pronunciation: ISH-ma-ell. Hebrew pronunciation: yish-mah-AYL.* Ishmael is a "sentence name" and means "God listened." He was born to Abram and Sarai's Egyptian maidservant Hagar. Abram was 86 years old when Ishmael was born. When Ishmael was 13 years old, God told Abraham that the males in his household should be circumcised, and Abraham complied. One year later Isaac was born. Twice God miraculously intervened to preserve Ishmael's life. Ishmael lived to be 137 years old. His

Isaac

descendants were called Ishmaelites—Arab tribes that were camel breeders and traders.

**JORDAN RIVER—**

*American English pronunciation: JOR-dan. Hebrew pronunciation: yar-DAYN. Greek pronunciation: yor-DAH-nays.* The Jordan River begins with four streams forming in the snow fields of Mount Hermon and ends up flowing through Palestine through Lake Huleh, then the Sea of Galilee, and finally to the Dead Sea, which has no outlet. It is the world's lowest river, most of the time flowing below sea level and meandering for nearly 200 miles, although a straight line would be only about 70 miles long. It typically floods in the spring. Depending on precipitation, some 8 to 35 billion cubic feet of water flow through the Jordan River each year. The Romans constructed the first bridge to span the river. Prior to that people had to cross it at one of the 60 or so fording places.

**LOT—***American English pronunciation: LOT. Hebrew pronunciation: LOHT.* Lot was the son of Abraham's brother Haran. The Bible indicates that Lot went with Abram on the trip to Canaan, which was not in harmony with God's directives to Abram to leave his family behind. Perhaps Abram saw his nephew as his possible heir, since he and Sarai were childless. Several times the Bible speaks of Lot in terms that make it sound as though he was a tagalong: "Abram . . . and Lot . . . with him." Lot owned large flocks and had many servants. When Abram's and Lot's herders began feuding over grazing and watering rights, the two men parted ways. Abraham let Lot choose which direction he wanted to move. Lot chose the Jordan Valley. When God decided to destroy the city of Sodom, Lot, his wife, and two unmarried daughters fled Sodom, but his wife turned around to look at Sodom and turned into a pillar of salt.

**MESOPOTAMIA—***American English pronunciation: mess-oh-poh-TAYM-ee-ah.* Mesopotamia is a Greek word that means "between the rivers." The two rivers implied in the name are the Euphrates on the west and

Lot

Noah

the Tigris on the east. Modern Iraq covers much of what was ancient Mesopotamia. The area encompasses wide geographic conditions—from desert to forests to floodplains. The Old Testament writers refer to it as *Aram-naharaim*. It was home to the ancient nations of the Sumerians, Akkadians, Amorites, Assyrians, and Babylonians. Writing was invented here in 3500 B.C., and it was here that the hour was divided into 60 minutes. Abram and Sarai emigrated from Mesopotamia to Canaan at God's command.

**MORIAH**—*American English pronunciation: mor-EYE-ah. Hebrew pronunciation: mor-ee-YAH.* Moriah was the place where Abraham went to offer Isaac as a burnt offering to Yahweh. The Bible says that it was a three-day journey from Beersheba, where Abraham was living. Biblical scholars are not sure whether to take the expression "three-day journey" literally or perhaps metaphorically, referring to a long trip. It has often been identified with the Temple Mount in Jerusalem. Today the Al-Aqsa Mosque

and the Dome of the Rock, the third holiest Islamic place, are situated on what may have been Mount Moriah. Muslims believe that Muhammad went to heaven from the spot the Dome of the Rock covers.

**NOAH**—*American English pronunciation: NOH-ah. Hebrew pronunciation: NO-akh.* The name Noah means "rest." Two persons in the Old Testament have the name Noah—a woman and a man. The person mentioned in this book is Noah, the son of Lamech. God asked Noah, a righteous man, to build the ark. The boat Noah built was 450 feet long, 75 feet wide, and 45 feet high. (The *Mayflower* was 90 feet long. The *Queen Mary* is 1,019.5 feet long. The *Titanic* was 882.5 feet in length.) When God first told Noah about the forthcoming flood, Noah was 480 years old. He was 600 years old when the Flood came. Many animals rode out the storm in the ark with Noah and his family. Seven pairs of clean animals (sheep and cows, for example) and two pairs of unclean animals (pigs and camels, for example) went into the ark. The ark floated on the

Sarah/Sarai

water for about a year. Noah died at age 950. He is the first recorded person to have planted a vineyard. According to the biblical account, all people on earth today are descendants of Noah's three sons: Shem, Ham, and Japheth.

**PERIZZITES**—*American English pronunciation: PEHR-iz-zites. Hebrew pronunciation: hap-pe-riz-ZEE.* The name may mean "rustic." It refers to a group of people who lived in Canaan as far back as the time of Abraham. In contrast to the Canaanites, who lived in walled cities, the Perizzites appear to have lived in the countryside. Because of this, the word, which always appears in Old Testament Hebrew with the definite article "the," may not refer to a specific ethnic group, but instead may be a generic term that refers to anyone living outside the fortified cities of Canaan. (The Latin word for "pagan," for example, referred not to a specific ethnic or religious group but to those who lived in the rural countryside.) They and the Canaanites appear to have been the two main groups of indigenous peoples occupying the land that God promised to Abraham and his offspring. During the time of Joshua the Perizzites lived in the mountainous areas of Palestine. Little is known of these people, and scholars are not sure how to identify them. Later King Solomon enslaved them.

**SARAH**—*American English pronunciation: SAIR-ah. Hebrew pronunciation: sah-RAH.* Sarah was the half sister and wife of Abraham, daughter of Terah with another wife. (Endogamous marriages—marriage to close relatives—was considered desirable in the ancient Near East. Pharaohs sometimes married their own daughters. Marriage to cousins was quite common.) She was about 10 years younger than Abraham and was barren for most of her life. She was about 65 years old when Abraham moved his household from Haran. When she was 90, she gave birth to Isaac. Sarah was legendary for her beauty—even in her old age—and two rulers wanted her in their harem. She died at Hebron (also called Kiriath-arba) when she was 127 years old. Abraham buried her in the Cave of Machpelah.

**SARAI**—*American English pronunciation: SAHR-eye. Hebrew pronunciation: sah-EYE.* Originally Abram's wife's name was Sarai, which God changed to Sarah when she was 89 years old—just a year prior to the time she gave birth to Isaac. Both the names Sarah and Sarai are closely related to each other and mean "princess."

**SHECHEM**—*American English pronunciation: SHECK-em. Hebrew pronunciation: shee-KEM.* In the Old Testament Shechem is the name of three people and a city. The term in this book refers to a walled Canaanite city in central Palestine. It was situated about 40 miles north of Jerusalem and covered nearly six acres of land. The name itself means something like "back" or "shoulder." The city was located in the natural pass between mounts Ebal and Gerizim. It was the first city in Canaan Abram stopped at after he left Haran. The donkey was a sacred animal of the city and was offered as a sacrifice there. The god

Baal-berith was worshipped here. Joseph was buried here. Archaeologists claim that they have found evidence that people lived in Shechem as early as around 4500 B.C. When the Hebrew people left Egypt and began taking over the land of Canaan, Shechem fell to them early on. It was here where Joshua renewed the covenant with the people, the covenant God initiated originally at Mount Sinai. During the time of the judges, a temple to Baal-berith (Baal of the covenant) was situated in Shechem. During part of its early history, a temple fortress was constructed inside Shechem. This new building had walls 17 feet thick! This temple existed for many years and appears to be the one mentioned in Judges 9 as the temple of Baal-berith. At the outset of the divided kingdom, Shechem served at first as Israel's capital city, which later was moved to nearby Samaria. In 750 B.C., during the time of the prophet Hosea, Shechem housed a shrine where Yahweh was worshipped. In 722 B.C. the Assyrians razed Shechem, but in 350 B.C. it was rebuilt. John Hyrcanus destroyed it permanently in 107 B.C. There

Shechem Middle Bronze wall

is still a city by that name. However, the site of ancient Shechem is located nearby at *Tell Balâtah*.

**SODOM**—*American English pronunciation: SAW-dum. Hebrew pronunciation: s'DOHM.* Sodom, the name means "field" or "burning" or "enclosed space," was one of five cities (Sodom, Gomorrah, Admah, Zeboiim, and Zoar) on the plain near the Dead Sea. After Lot and Abram parted ways, Lot pitched his tent toward Sodom. Later we find him living in the city and sitting in its gate. God incinerated the city, along with Gomorrah, because of its wickedness. But He sent angels to evacuate Lot and his family. The people who lived in this city-state were known as Sodomites. Archaeologists are not sure of the location of ancient Sodom. Some people think that it may be under the waters of the Dead Sea. Others speculate that it was situated elsewhere. For example, some think the twin cities of Sodom and Gomorrah were at the northern end of the Dead Sea, by the mouth of the Jordan River. Others are convinced that they were at the south end of the Dead Sea,

where Har-sodom—Mount Sodom—is located.

**TERAH**—*American English pronunciation: TAY-rah. Hebrew pronunciation: TAIR-akh.* The proper name Terah is used in the Bible to refer to a man and a place. The Terah in this book was the son of a man called Nahor and the father of Abram, Nahor (perhaps named after his grandfather), and Haran. The name Terah probably means "ibex," a mountain goat, although some scholars have seen in the name an allusion to the moon god. Terah—and probably his family—served "other gods," one of whom was most likely Sin, the moon god of Ur and Haran. The rabbis identified Terah as someone who both made and worshipped idols. At some point Terah moved his household from Ur to Haran. Terah was 205 years old when he died.

**UR**—*American English pronunciation: UHR. Hebrew pronunciation: OOR.* Ur of the Chaldees is the city in southern Mesopotamia from

Lot's wife was turned into a pillar of salt when Sodom was destroyed.

which Terah and his household immigrated to Haran in northern Mesopotamia. It was one of the oldest cities in ancient southern Mesopotamia. Some archaeologists believe that the city was inhabited as early as 5500 B.C. The name of the first king of Ur (at least, the first name we know) was Mes-Anni-Padda. Ur covered nearly 67 acres. The city was located about 140 miles south of Babylon. From at least c. 3000 B.C. Ur was an important center for the worship of the moon god Sin, or Nanna (sometimes spelled Nannar). Just prior to 2000 B.C., around the time of Terah, the Elamites conquered and destroyed Ur. He and his household may have been living in the vicinity of Haran at this time. The ancient location of the city is now called *Tell el-Muqayyar* and is about 10 miles west of the Euphrates River. Originally the city was situated on the banks of the Euphrates, but since that time the river has changed its course. Archaeologists found many treasured objects during their excavations of Ur.

**ZOAR**—*American English pronunciation: ZOH-ar. Hebrew pronunciation:*

Ur

*TSOH-ar.* Zoar was a village not too far from Sodom. In Abram's time King Bela ruled Zoar, or perhaps the city was also known as Bela. When the angels told Lot and his family to flee Sodom and actually pushed or dragged them through the city gate, Lot begged them to let him take shelter in Zoar rather than in the hills. The angels allowed him to do that. There is some evidence that later on in history Zoar was under the control of the Moabites, one clan that had descended from

Lot's incestuous relationship with his daughter. The exact location of Zoar remains problematical. Some authorities believe that it was situated in the southernmost point of the Jordan Valley. Some speculate that it may have been located near the mountains of Moab, where there is still a large oasis, which may have been even bigger in ancient times. There is other biblical evidence that puts it within visible distance of the Valley of Jericho, which would situate it at the north end of the Dead Sea.

# RUTH REDDING BRAND

Ruth Redding Brand, assistant professor of English at Atlantic Union College in Massachusetts, has written the main stories in this book. Bible stories have fascinated her from the time she was a child. When the Review and Herald Publishing Association invited her to explore the Holy Land with the late Siegfried Horn, a world-renowned archaeologist and eminently knowledgeable tour guide, she eagerly accepted. That experience (along with a lot of research) gave her access to an authenticity of detail that makes the narratives in the Family Bible Story books live and breathe.

FINKLE PHOTOGRAPHY

Brand was raised on a dairy farm in Maine and grew up milking cows, haying, riding hefty workhorses, and pulling weeds in acres of corn and cucumbers. As an adult she has taught elementary school and junior high as well as college. Since earning her Master's degree in English, she has taught English at Fitchburg State College and Atlantic Union College.

She lives in Lancaster, Massachusetts, with her husband, Bob, and pampered cat, Sky. She is blessed with two adult children, Jeffrey and Heidi, and their respective spouses, Krista (Motschiedler) and Troy Clark. Brand loves to read, play word games, walk on the beach, and swim, but she'll drop any of these activities in a heartbeat to spend time with her granddaughter, little Miss Emma Mae Clark!

# LINDA PORTER CARLYLE

Linda Porter Carlyle, who wrote the Bible bedtime stories for this book, says, "I love the poetry and the music of words. I especially take pleasure in writing read-aloud stories for the very young."

Carlyle lives with her husband, two beautiful daughters, one dog, three cats, and two rabbits on a quiet dead-end, tree-lined street. She homeschools her children, Sarah and Abby.

Among her favorite things are paper and pencils and pens and pens. She also savors the quietness of a library,

the smell of books, the feel of their pages, and the way the words look printed there.

Linda Porter Carlyle hopes that parents and children will be able to cuddle close to each other and enjoy—again and again—these Bible bedtime stories together. These stories also provide good exercises for beginning readers.

# LEONA GLIDDEN RUNNING

Even as a little girl, Leona Glidden Running found foreign languages fascinating. In high school she learned Spanish from an older student who taught her during lunchtime. In college she majored in French and minored in German, which she later taught at the high school level.

For four years Running worked for the Voice of Prophecy, a well-known religious radiobroadcast originating from California, where she typed scripts in Spanish and Portuguese. During that time her husband, Leif (Bud) Running, died. She felt as though she were in a tunnel for eight years. Then she fell seriously ill, and when she recovered Running attended seminary, where she learned biblical Greek and Hebrew. From there she began teaching seminary classes in biblical languages while she worked on a doctorate in Semitic languages at Johns Hopkins University.

For many years Running taught ancient languages at Andrews University in Michigan. Even after her retirement she taught Egyptian hieroglyphics, Assyrian/Babylonian cuneiform, and ancient Syriac for 21 more years. Today Running enjoys total retirement from the classroom. She encourages young people with these words: "Find your gift, develop it, and let God use it!"

Leona Glidden Running reviewed for accuracy the stories in the Family Bible Story series. She also prepared the pronunciation guide at the end of this book.

# CONSTANCE CLARK GANE

Born in Brunswick, Maine, Connie moved with her parents (Richard and Virginia Clark) to the mission field when she was only 6 years old. She lived for nine years in Nepal, followed by two years in Pune, India.

Gane attended Pacific Union College, where in 1986 she received her bachelor's degree in music with an emphasis in violin. For the next two years she and her husband, Roy, lived in Israel, where they studied at the Hebrew University in Jerusalem.

Her University of California, at Berkeley M.A. and Ph.D. degrees are in Mesopotamian archaeology. Gane has participated in archaeological excavations at Tel Dor and Tel Dan in Israel, the ancient site of Nineveh in Iraq, and Tal Jalul in Jordan. Her area of general interest is that of the ancient Near East under the dominance of the Neo-Assyrian, Neo-Babylonian, and Achaemenid empires. Specifically she specializes in *Mischwesesn*, composite creatures, found in Late Neo-Babylonian religious art.

Gane currently is assistant professor of archaeology and Old Testament at the Seventh-day Adventist Theological Seminary at Andrews University in Berrien Springs, Michigan. She and her husband are the parents of one daughter, Sarah Elizabeth. Sarah keeps her parents in touch with reality and constantly turns their eyes and hearts to Jesus Christ.

# JOHN WHITE

John White is an accomplished commercial and historical illustrator with 20 years of experience in the industry. His clients include Zondervan Publishing, Osprey Publishing, Baker Book House, Ingersoll-Rand, Siemens, and Bank of America. His artwork has won awards from several organizations, including the Charlotte Society of Communication Arts and the Broadcast Design Association.

White's love of history inspires him to re-create pivotal events of the past. His painting *Sinking of the Battleship* Yamato won second place in a nationwide competition at the National Museum of Naval Aviation in Pensacola, Florida. He says, "History is our link to the past and our inspiration on where to go in the future. I like to take an actual historical event and portray it as accurately and dynamically as possible. I want those who view my paintings to enter vicariously into the story being told and to experience the event as a participant. When I accomplish that, I know I have done a good job."

White's historical illustrations have appeared in *Aviation History Magazine* and *Aviation Art Magazine* as well as on the History Channel.

John White and his wife, Margery, live in Charlotte, North Carolina. They greatly enjoy their two cats, Skittles and Anna Belle. The Whites enjoy traveling, gardening, working out at the gym, water sports, art shows, and church. John is a Sunday school teacher, and Margery tends the nursery.

The development of each of the pieces of artwork in this book goes through a certain process. John White went through various rough sketches as he refined his vision of Abraham sacrificing Isaac. All of his work is submitted to an oversight committee that reviews them and makes suggestions for possible improvements.

Here we see an electronic composite of his tight sketch and the final rendering.

# DARREL TANK

One of Darrel Tank's earliest memories of art is drawing pictures with his mother. She encouraged his creativity, which was apparent even when he was a very small child. While growing up, he often spent his afternoons at the publishing house where his father was the head photographer. The work of the illustrators there particularly fascinated him, and he began to dream of pursuing a career in art.

Tank was able to accomplish that dream in the late seventies and has exhibited and received honors at numerous art shows with his sensitive approach to portraiture. His photo-realistic style shows remarkable attention to fine detail and captures the emotion of the moment.

Tank and his wife, Denise, have four children and 12 grandchildren. They live in Garden Valley, Idaho, up in the mountains where they have snow for three to four months of the year. He writes, "We are sur-rounded by meadows, forests of pines and firs, and groves of aspens. There's a tremendous amount of wildlife, including herds of elk and deer, foxes, bears, mountain lions, wild turkeys, bald eagles, raccoons, Canada geese, and so much more."

The Tanks have an "extremely smart" yellow Labrador retriever named Chamois. She knows many tricks and loves to perform them for visitors. They also have two cats. One is 13 years old and is named Sienna, because of her color. The other is a pure white, long-haired cat.

Tank's repertoire includes black-and-white pencil renderings, color pencil, gouache, airbrush paintings, and computer illustrations, which have appeared in more than 400 books, magazines, advertising, and prints.

Darrel Tank goes through many steps before completing his pencil illustrations. He has to select models and have them photographed in their specific poses. He frequently has biblical attire specially made for his models, which helps him make the image look more realistic.

The image to the left is an electronic composite of Darrel's initial sketch and the finished image.

# ACKNOWLEDGMENTS

**W**here does one begin? So many individuals have helped in the construction of this unique book. We owe all a great debt of gratitude for the time and effort they invested to make the book a reality. Perhaps we can talk in categories of influence.

## RESEARCH

*Gail Hunt,* who had the first vision of a multilayer book and then conducted 11 focus groups around the United States

*Richard W. Coffen,* who brainstormed with Mr. Hunt and became director of the project

*Gerald Wheeler,* who as a Bible lover and book editor embraced the concept

*Patricia Fritz,* who spent many hours coordinating myriads of details

*Bob Haddock and Associates,* who helped with early marketing plans

The **many men and women and boys and girls** who shared their valuable ideas at the focus groups

## ADMINISTRATION

*Harold F. Otis, Jr.,* president who caught the vision immediately

*Robert S. Smith,* president who insisted on moving ahead after years of delay

*Hepsiba S. Singh,* treasurer who offered the financial support needed

*Mark B. Thomas,* vice president of the Book Division, who helped facilitate development and chaired our oversight committee

*Jeannette Johnson,* acquisitions editor, who kept minutes for the oversight committee

*Trent Truman,* art coordinator, who prepared the layout and design and worked with the talented illustrators who provided such amazing artwork

## WRITERS

*Ruth Redding Brand,* who researched and wrote the main stories in this series

*Linda Porter Carlyle and Heather Grovet,* who wrote the Bedtime Bible Stories

*Constance Clark Gane,* who prepared the time lines

*Leona Glidden Running,* who prepared the pronunciation guide in the glossary/Bible dictionary

*Richard W. Coffen and Gerald Wheeler,* who wrote the Did You Know? sections

## ILLUSTRATIVE ENDEAVORS

John White      Darrel Tank

## YOUNG READERS

| | | | | |
|---|---|---|---|---|
| Benjamin Baker | Nathan Blake | Annalise Harvey | Katrina Pepper | Bradley Thomas |
| David Baker | Coramina Cogan | Alyssa Harvey | Lisa Sayler | Jeremy Tooley |
| Emily Barr | Raeven Cogan | Garrick Herr | Emily Shockey | Tara Van Hyning |
| Jacob Barr | Rande Colburn | Alicia O'Connor | Katie Shockey | Kim Wasenmiller |
| Carin Bartlett | Zoë Rose Fritz | Jeremy Pepper | Jonathan Singh | Tompaul Wheeler |
| Caitlyn Bartlett | Jennifer Hanson | Jessica Pepper | Kaitlyn Singh | Megan Williams |

## SCHOLARLY INPUT

| | | | |
|---|---|---|---|
| *Douglas Clark* | *Siegfried Horn* | *Pedrito Maynard-Reid* | *Warren Trenchard* |
| *Larry Herr* | *John R. Jones* | *Leona Glidden Running* | *S. Douglas Waterhouse* |
| *Lawrence T. Geraty* | *Sakae Kubo* | *Ronald Springett* | *Randall Younker* |

## LITERARY INPUT

*Denise Herr,* college English teacher

*Kelly Bird,* college student of Ms. Herr

*Orval Driskel,* marketer

*Tracy Fry,* college student of Ms. Herr

*Susan Harvey,* marketer

*Eugene Lincoln,* editor

*Donna Martens,* college student of Ms. Herr

*Shelley Pocha,* college student of Ms. Herr

*Sherry Rusk,* college student of Ms. Herr

*Sandy Robinson,* marketer

*Sheri Rusk,* college student of Ms. Herr

*Doug Sayles,* marketer

*Gerald Wheeler,* editor

*Penny Wheeler,* editor

*Ray Woolsey,* editor

## EDITORIAL HELP

*Eugene Lincoln,* who helped edit and copyedit early versions

*Delma Miller,* copy editor

*James Cavil,* copy editor

*Jocelyn Fay,* copy editor

## MISCELLANEOUS HELP

*Tompaul Wheeler,* resource coordinator